Teens, Libraries, and Social Networking

TEENS, LIBRARIES, AND SOCIAL NETWORKING

What Librarians Need to Know

Denise E. Agosto and
June Abbas, Editors

Libraries Unlimited Professional Guides for Young
Adult Librarians Series
C. Allen Nichols and Mary Anne Nichols, Series Editors

AN IMPRINT OF ABC-CLIO, LLC
Santa Barbara, California • Denver, Colorado • Oxford, England

Library of Congress Cataloging-in-Publication Data

Teens, libraries, and social networking : what librarians need to know /
Denise E. Agosto and June Abbas, editors.
        p. cm. — (Recent titles in libraries unlimited professional guides for young
adult librarians)
    Includes index.
    ISBN 978-1-59884-575-4 (hard copy : alk. paper) — ISBN 978-1-59884-576-1
(ebook)   1. Libraries and teenagers—United States.   2. Internet in young
adults' libraries—United States.   3. Online social networks—United States.
I. Agosto, Denise E.   II. Abbas, June, 1964–
    Z718.5.T446   2011
    027.62'6—dc22   2011004690

ISBN: 978-1-59884-575-4
EISBN: 978-1-59884-576-1

15   14   13   12   11   1   2   3   4   5

This book is also available on the World Wide Web as an eBook.
Visit www.abc-clio.com for details.

Libraries Unlimited
An Imprint of ABC-CLIO, LLC

ABC-CLIO, LLC
130 Cremona Drive, P.O. Box 1911
Santa Barbara, California 93116-1911

This book is printed on acid-free paper (∞)

Manufactured in the United States of America

For David and Rachel, the stars of my own personal social network
DEA

For Clifford and Ben, my very own teen informants.
JA

CONTENTS

SERIES FOREWORD

We firmly believe that teens should be provided with equal access to library services and that those services should be equal to those offered to other library customers. This series supports that belief. We are very excited about *Teens, Libraries, and Social Networking: What Librarians Need to Know* as the newest addition to our series. Denise Agosto and June Abbas have written and edited a comprehensive survey of this topic, which is so very important and popular with teens. You will find this information, supported by the authors' own research and the expertise of those working in the field, indispensable as you tackle the issues in your library.

We are proud of our association with Libraries Unlimited/ABC-CLIO, which continues to prove itself as the premier publisher of books to help library staff serve teens. This series has succeeded because our authors know the needs of those library employees who work with young adults. Without exception, they have written useful and practical handbooks for library staff.

We hope that you will find this book, as well as our entire series, informative, providing you with valuable ideas as you serve teens, and that this work will further inspire you to do great things to make teens welcome in your library. If you have an idea for a title that could be added to our series or would like to submit a book proposal, please email us at lu-books@lu.com. We'd love to hear from you.

Mary Anne Nichols
C. Allen Nichols

INTRODUCTION: TEENS, LIBRARIES, AND ONLINE SOCIAL NETWORKS: A NEW ERA FOR LIBRARY SERVICES TO YOUNG ADULTS

Denise E. Agosto and
June Abbas

Many of today's teens spend hours each day on Facebook, MySpace, Twitter, and other online social networks, but what does this mean for public library services to young adults? This book explains the reasons why so many teens use these tools and offers suggestions as to how best to use them to serve teens, both online and in the library. It also examines issues of critical concern to librarians and parents, such as safety and privacy issues, and analyzes the social and educational benefits of online social networking.

Online social networks began in the late 1990s, gaining widespread popularity and media coverage in 2003 (Boyd 2007). In just the few short years since then, millions of teens have joined these sites. But what are online social networks, and why do so many teens use them? Simply put, social networking sites are online spaces where community members meet to engage in all kinds of social interactions, from reading about other members, to posting pictures and video clips, to sending messages to online friends.

As our own research and the research of many others has shown, the number one reason why teens use social networks is to keep in touch with friends (see, e.g., Agosto and Abbas 2009; Boyd 2007; Bumgarner 2007; Ito et al. 2008; Lenhart et al. 2007; and Subrahmanyam and Greenfield 2008).

Usually these are friends known first in the "offline" world, but sometimes teens do meet new people online, usually by "friending" friends of friends. To get started in most social networking sites, a user creates an account and sets up a personal profile, or "page." Typically only a small portion of a person's page is open for public viewing, most commonly the user's name and photograph. Users can add details about hobbies, interests, education, and much more. Many users also join groups to support causes, express political viewpoints, or express personal interests, such as the Facebook group Teen Trash Novels. Teen Trash Novels describes itself as being "For all those times you have gone to your bookshelf, thinking you'll read a quality adult novel such as *The Kite Runner*, and end up re-reading *The Princess Diaries* or *Gossip Girl* . . . again for the 5th time."

After creating an account and a profile, users can invite people to become their "friends." Friending someone typically enables both friends to see the full content of each other's pages and to post comments on each other's pages as well. Users receive status updates when their friends change their pages, add new content such as pictures and video clips, join new interest groups, and so on. Many teens check their pages daily to learn the latest news and gossip about their online friends.

While the popular press has often portrayed social networking sites as dominated by teens, most of the biggest sites have as many or more adult members as teen members. Two of the biggest are MySpace and Facebook, each with roughly 200 million registered users worldwide. In the United States, Facebook replaced MySpace in 2009 as the most popular social network. In June of that year, roughly 77 million unique U.S. users visited Facebook and about 68.5 million unique U.S. users visited MySpace (Rao 2009). At both of these sites, adults comprise the majority of the registered users. In 2007, Thelwall (2008) found the median age of MySpace users to be 21, with slightly more female than male users. And as of July 2009, Facebook reported that its fastest-growing user group was adults aged 35 and older.

Still, social networking is undeniably widespread among U.S. teens. A 2010 Pew Internet & American Life Project survey found that of the 93% of U.S. teens (ages 12 to 17) who go online, nearly three-quarters (73%) use social networking sites (Lenhart et al. 2010). It seems that the use of social networks is more widespread among teens than adults. A 2009 Harris poll found 48% of adult U.S. respondents to have a Facebook or MySpace account. Of those in the youngest group polled, 18- to 34-year-olds, 74% of U.S. respondents had an account on one or both of these sites. In the oldest group polled, those ages 55 and older, just 24% had an account (Harris 2009).

DEFINING "SOCIAL NETWORKS" AND "SOCIAL NETWORKING" WITHIN THE CONTEXT OF THIS BOOK

Strictly speaking, an online social network is a digital space that enables users to register, create personal profiles, select whom to "friend" within the community, and communicate with and share content with online friends. A well-known example of a social network that is popular with teens is Facebook. Teens use Facebook to create online identities and to communicate with friends, family, and other members of their social worlds.

Social networks are often confused with social media. Social media are digital tools designed more for digital content sharing and less for purposes of communication and interaction. YouTube is a popular social media tool and one that many teens use for sharing videos. Within You-Tube, users can comment on other users' videos, but the main purpose of the site is content sharing. Thus, a defining difference between social networks and social media is bidirectional information sharing and interaction (social networks) versus unidirectional information broadcasting (social media). In practice, however, there are often overlaps between the kinds of interactions taking places in social networks and social media.

We take a broad approach to defining *social networks* and *social networking* within the context of this book. Although content-sharing sites such as YouTube and tool-building platforms such as Nings are not true social networks in the strict definition of the term, they are included in this book because they offer useful ways of using digital tools to connect with teens online. (Nings and how they can be used to provide services to teens are explained further in chapter 5.) Many of the chapters move beyond thinking just about how to leverage social networks for the delivery of library services to teens to thinking about how to use social networks, social media, and other useful digital tools as well. The goal of serving teens in the best ways possible is really the key here, much more so than limiting our discussions to true social networking technologies.

HOW DO PUBLIC LIBRARIES USE ONLINE SOCIAL NETWORKS TO DELIVER SERVICES TO TEENS?

Recognizing that social networking sites are where the teens are, many public libraries have entered the world of online social networking. Each of these libraries uses social networks in slightly different ways, but common uses include posting information about new book and media purchases, advertising library programs and events, and providing reference and readers' advisory via the sites' instant messaging (IM) or e-mail systems.

For example, the young adult department of the Park Ridge Public Library in Park Ridge, Illinois, has a Facebook page. As of February 2011, a total of 369 Facebook members, many of whom were teen library users, had indicated that they liked the page. (In April 2010, the Facebook "like" button replaced the old "fan" button.) The page links to the library's website, to the young adult (YA) department's website, to the YA department's book blog, and to a book blog written by teens. It also provides basic contact information for the library; posts the Park Ridge Library Young Adult Loft's feed of book, music, movie, and game reviews; advertises forthcoming library programs; and posts pictures of past programs.

The Worthington Libraries Teen MySpace page has similar content. It offers descriptions of library services; a teen blog; and music, movie, and book suggestions. As of February 2011, there were 822 friends of the MySpace page, and again, many were teen library users. A number of teens had written on the page, thanking library staff for presenting programs, posting titles of their favorite YA books, and more.

Other library systems have even larger lists of teen fans and friends online. For example, the Loft at ImaginOn was an early adopter of social networks. A joint collaboration of the Children's Theatre of Charlotte and the Public Library of Charlotte-Mecklenburg County (North Carolina), the Loft at ImaginOn maintains a highly active MySpace page with 1,026 friends as of February 2011. The page features video clips, a weekly top 10 music playlist, book recommendations, a community blog, a computer gaming blog, information about library programs and events, and more.

More and more libraries are moving toward serving teens via social media and social networks. Many libraries are moving toward integrating these tools into their services within the physical library. The Chicago Public Library, for example, has had success in engaging teens with its YouMedia online community. Within the library:

> The Digital Space offers eight desktop computers, 96 laptops, two PlayStation 3's with a library of games, and musical keyboards and a recording studio so teenagers can create music, art and poetry, or jump online and talk with peers in the secure, password-protected YOUMedia forum. (Guy 2010)

It is a space for technical education, creative exploration, and multimedia arts appreciation. Teens are also encouraged to post book reviews and to talk about books online, connecting more traditional library activities with newer technology-based activities.

OVERVIEW OF THE BOOK

As we have pointed out above, social networking is a growing trend that is especially popular with teens. Why would public libraries want to be a part of this trend? In an article we published in the journal *Public Libraries* in the May/June 2009 issue, we reviewed the research literature relating to teens, librarians, and social networks and concluded that public libraries can benefit from their use in a three major ways: (1) by broadening the reach of the library's YA programs and services, (2) by enabling the library to better support teens' healthy social development, and (3) by facilitating opportunities for public librarians to teach teens how to engage in safer online interactions (Agosto and Abbas 2009).

This book explains these three categories of benefits of using social networks to connect with teens in more detail and describes specific ways in which public librarians can obtain these benefits for their libraries. We also address the potential drawbacks. The chapter authors are professors who conduct research with teens and their use of libraries and YA librarians and school librarians who are leaders in the use of social networks to deliver library services. Together, the chapters provide an in-depth overview of what librarians need to know about online social networks in order to best serve their teen communities.

In chapter 1, "What Do Public Librarians Really *Do* with Social Networking? Profiles of Five Public Libraries," we summarize two recent studies of public libraries' use of social networks to explain what researchers know about how public libraries use these tools to serve teens. We then take a closer look at five such libraries, ranging from a large urban library to a small suburban library, to show which technologies each library uses and the kinds of services and programs offered using these tools. Together the two studies and the five library profiles show that although there has been a small trend for public libraries moving into the social networking arena, it is a fairly small trend, and even those libraries that do use social networks are doing so for a limited range of purposes.

We present another of our studies in chapter 2, "Looking Closely at Teens' Use of Social Networks: What Do High School Seniors Do Online?" Along with Joyce Kasman Valenza, a school librarian working in a suburban Philadelphia school, we have recently completed work on a series of focus group interviews with seniors in a highly technological suburban high school. This chapter describes the study and explains what the results can teach us about how teens use information and communication technologies in both their private and school lives and what these behaviors mean for library services to young adults.

In chapter 3, "How Social Networking Sites Aid in Teen Development," Sean Rapacki, a teen services librarian, challenges the common perception that teens are wasting their time using social networks. Not only do teens derive entertainment from social networking, but there are a host of social and educational benefits that teens can derive from using them as well. The author first outlines some of teens' developmental needs. He then shows how librarians can use social networks to deliver library programs and services that can maximize developmental benefits for their YA patrons.

Next, Belinha De Abreu addresses the concept of media literacy in chapter 4, "The Role of Media Literacy Education within Social Networking and the Library." She first explains that media literacy is "the ability to access, analyze, evaluate, and communicate information in a variety of forms and formats," and she then explains why being media literate is crucial for today's students. She moves on to show how social networks are particularly fertile environments for teaching teens to become media literate and why librarians should work with educators and with teens themselves to promote media literacy among young adults.

From Facebook to MySpace to Nings to blogs, the number and range of available social networks, social media, and other online tools is enormous and growing. With so many different options to choose from, it can be difficult for librarians to know which tools are right for their particular needs. Stephanie D. Reynolds, in chapter 5, offers "If You Build It, Will They Come? A Comparison of Social Networking Utilities" to help make these selection decisions easier. She profiles a number of the leading online tools and teaches librarians how to choose the best technologies to meet their programming and service goals.

In chapter 6, "Teens, Social Networking, and Safety and Privacy Issues," we address issues of safety and privacy in social networks and other online environments. Some librarians and parents are hesitant to support teens' use of online social networks, and much of this resistance comes from worries about teens' safety and privacy online. We summarize the research into teens' online safety and privacy to show that the popular media have often exaggerated the dangers of social network use. We then suggest methods for teaching teens how to be smarter and safer users of these tools.

Not only are safety and privacy issues important considerations in offering library services via social networks, legal issues must also be taken into account. Annette Lamb provides a brief primer of related laws and regulations in chapter 7, "Social Networking: Teen Rights, Responsibilities, and Legal Issues." She uses simple, plain language to explain these laws to nonexperts and to teach librarians what they need to know in order to implement such laws properly within their libraries.

Promoting reading has been a fundamental purpose of YA library services since public libraries first began serving teens. In chapter 8, "Using Social Networking Sites to Connect Teens with Young Adult Literature," Janet Hilbun shows us how librarians can mix traditional library services for teens with new modes of online information delivery to help promote teen reading. Indeed, one of the most popular ways that public libraries use online social networks is to promote teen fiction reading. This chapter offers specific tips for using social networking sites to connect teens to YA literature, such as introducing teens to YA fiction blogs, online book clubs and literature circles, book-sharing sites, and more.

Chapter 9 provides still more examples of exciting new ways in which librarians can use social networks to promote reading and the love of literature. In "Fandom as a Form of Social Networking," Elizabeth Burns investigates the fascinating world of online fandoms. Fandoms are online communities built around a book, movie, song, or other creative work. The chapter profiles a number of popular teen fandoms, from Harry Potter communities to fan sites for popular YA authors, and teaches librarians how to use fandoms and fan activities like fan fiction writing to get teens excited about reading and writing.

Next, Eric M. Meyers gives us a peek into the future of library services for young adults. In chapter 10, "Hanging Out on the Grid: Virtual Worlds for Teens and Preteens," he explores online virtual worlds for teens, such as Teen Second Life, Habbo Hotel, and Gaia. He discusses the differences between virtual games and virtual worlds and explains how virtual worlds support online identity building, literacy development, problem-solving skills, and community membership for teens.

All of the ideas discussed in the previous chapters come together in chapter 11, "Pages, Profiles, and Podcasts: How Charlotte-Mecklenburg Library Engages Teens through Social Networking." In this chapter librarians Holly Summers, Rebecca Pierson, Christen Higgins, and Ralph Woodring show how the award-winning Charlotte-Mecklenburg Library serves teens via a number of social networking tools. Recently recognized by both the Institute for Museum and Library Services and *Library Journal* as a top U.S. public library, Charlotte-Mecklenburg Library was an early adopter of online social networking for teens and remains a leader in the field. This chapter describes the many innovative ways in which Charlotte-Mecklenburg Library uses these technologies to serve teens and stands as a model for other libraries to follow in moving their own teen library services deeper into the online world.

Finally, we conclude with chapter 12, "Bringing It All Together: What Does It Mean for Librarians Who Serve Teens?" With this final chapter, we summarize the main points made throughout the book to ensure that readers are left with an understanding of the most important issues and a concise list of pivotal suggestions for best practices. We focus not just on the success stories presented throughout the book but also on the not-so-successful ventures, so that other librarians can learn from these triumphs and mistakes as we all move further into this exciting new era of library services for teens.

REFERENCES

Agosto, Denise E., and June Abbas. "Teens and Social Networking: How Public Libraries Are Responding to the Latest Online Trend." *Public Libraries* 48 (2009): 32–37.

Boyd, Danah. "Why Youth (Heart) Social Network Sites: The Role of Networked Publics in Teenage Social Life." In *MacArthur Foundation Series on Digital Learning: Youth, Identity, and Digital Media*, edited by David Buckingham. Cambridge, MA: MIT Press, 2007.

Bumgarner, Brett A. "You Have Been Poked: Exploring the Uses and Gratifications of Facebook among Emerging Adults." *First Monday* 12 (2007): n.p., http://firstmonday.org/htbin/cgiwrap/bin/ojs/index.php/fm/article/view/2026/1897 (accessed March 10, 2010).

Guy, Sandra. "Library Site a Hot New Social Media Hangout for Teens." *Chicago Sun Times* (March 6, 2010), http://www.suntimes.com/technology/guy/2086682,CST-NWS-ECOL06.article (accessed March 10, 2010).

Harris Interactive. "Just under Half of Americans Have a Facebook or MySpace Account." April 16, 2009, http://www.harrisinteractive.com/harris_poll/pubs/Harris_Poll_2009_04_16.pdf (accessed March 10, 2010).

Ito, Mikuko, et al. "Living and Learning with New Media: Summary of Findings from the Digital Youth Project." *John D. and Catherine T. MacArthur Foundation Reports on Digital Media and Learning*, 2008, http://digitalyouth.ischool.berkeley.edu/report (accessed March 10, 2010).

Lenhart, Amanda, Mary Madden, Alexandra R. Macgill, and Aaron Smith. *Teens and Social Media*. Pew Research Center for the People & the Press, 2007, http://www.pewinternet.org/~/media/Files/Reports/2007/PIP_Teens_Social_Media_Final.pdf.pdf (accessed May 1, 2010).

Lenhart, Amanda, Kristen Purcell, Aaron Smith, and Kathryn Zickuhr. "Social Media and Young Adults." Pew Internet & American Life Project, http://pewinternet.org/Reports/2010/Social-Media-and-Young-Adults.aspx (accessed February 3, 2010).

Roa, Leena. "The Gap Grows Wider: MySpace Eats Facebook's Dust in the U.S." *Techcrunch,* 2009, http://www.techcrunch.com/2009/07/13/the-gap-grows-wider-myspace-eats-facebooks-dust-in-the-us (accessed February 18, 2010).

Subrahmanyam, Kaveri, and Patricia Greenfield. "Online Communication and Adolescent Relationships." *The Future of Children* 18 (2008): 119–46.

Thelwall, Mike. "Social Networks, Gender, and Friending: An Analysis of MySpace Member Profiles." *Journal of the American Society for Information Science* 59 (2008): 1321–30.

WEBSITES

Facebook user group information, http://www.facebook.com/press/info.php?statistics/

The Loft at ImaginOn MySpace page, http://www.myspace.com/libraryloft/

Park Ridge Public Library Facebook page, www.facebook.com/YALoft/

Worthington Libraries Teen MySpace page, www.myspace.com/worthingteens/

YouTube, http://www.youtube.com/

1

◈ ◈ ◈

WHAT DO PUBLIC LIBRARIANS REALLY *DO* WITH SOCIAL NETWORKING? PROFILES OF FIVE PUBLIC LIBRARIES

June Abbas and Denise E. Agosto

As we noted in the Introduction, social networking is a growing trend with teens. A 2010 Pew Internet & American Life Project survey found that of the 93% of U.S. teens ages 12 to 17 who go online, nearly three-quarters (73%) use social networking sites (Lenhart et al. 2010), compared with 72% for young adults ages 18 to 29 and 47% for adults. The Pew study also reported the different social networking technologies and activities favored by teens and their popularity with this group:

- 14% blog (down 50% from 2006).
- 8% use Twitter.
- 8% visit online virtual worlds.
- 38% share content online.
- 21% remix content (Lenhart et al. 2010).

Looking at these statistics, it is evident that teens are using social networking technologies. But what are the benefits to the libraries that use them to connect with teens? Why would public libraries want to be a part of this trend? In Agosto and Abbas (2009), we concluded that public libraries can benefit from the use of social networks with teens in a three major ways: (1) by broadening the reach of the library's young adult programs and services, (2) by enabling the library to better support teens' healthy social development, and (3) by facilitating opportunities for public librarians to teach teens how to engage in safer online interactions.

It seems like a win–win situation: teens are using social networks and libraries can benefit by using them to connect with their teen populations. But this question still remains: *"Are* public libraries actually using social networking technologies to provide services to teens?"

HOW U.S. PUBLIC LIBRARIES USE SOCIAL NETWORKS TO SERVE TEENS: TWO RECENT STUDIES

The professional literature is filled with explanations of different social networking technologies and good suggestions on how to use them to connect with teens. There are also many insightful accounts of specific libraries' uses of social networks for teen programming and services. Unfortunately, little research has been done that explores the prevalence of their general use among public libraries, let alone research that focuses on services for teens. We found just two studies that have begun to determine *how many* public libraries are using social networks with teens and also *how* they are using them. These two studies are outlined here.

Study 1

This study was conducted in the fall of 2007 by Robyn Lupa, Head of Children's Information Services of the Arvada Library of the Jefferson County Public Library, located in Arvada, Colorado. She used a survey to learn more about how librarians who serve young adults are using social networks with their teen populations. Lupa invited librarians to participate by posting a message on the PUBYAC, PUBLIB, and yalsa-bk e-mail lists. A total of 118 responses were gathered from libraries around the United States. (Unfortunately, no additional information on Lupa's methodology for the survey was reported, so we do not know any further details related to the libraries that responded—for example, their location and size or the type of library.) Some of the findings of this study included the following:

Are teens using social networking in the library, and why are they doing so?

- Librarians observed 91% of their teens using social networks on library computers.

- Gaming and virtual worlds were used by 78% of the teens.
- When asked their opinions on *why* teens used social networking sites, librarians reported the following reasons:
  - To show off, or for the "coolness" factor
  - To keep in touch with friends
  - To receive instant feedback on items they had posted online (such as pictures and comments)
  - To be "bold, expressive, and unrestrained in their communication"
  - Because of the ease of using the sites ("Proper spelling and grammar are not required!") (Lupa 2009, 99–100)

Are librarians using social networking with teens, and how?

- 61% of responding librarians who worked with teens had a MySpace or Facebook page of their own. Some of them used the sites to communicate with teens but also for themselves personally.
- 62% reported that their library or school did not have a presence on MySpace or Facebook, and they expressed frustration with their administrators or IT departments.
- Respondents who reported that their library or school had institutional pages on social networks shared a variety of positive and negative experiences in using them. For example:
  - Some of the survey respondents had found them to be effective for announcing programs, events, and services. Some used them for posting book reviews or for taking questions from teens.
  - Some reported that their social network pages were not frequently used by teens and that teens preferred to contact librarians directly or use librarians' personal pages instead of institutional pages.
  - Some of the librarians reported that updating library pages was relatively easy but could be time-consuming (Lupa 2009, 101–2).

What are some examples of how social networking is being used with teens?

- 21% of the responding librarians had used social networking sites to encourage reading, offer online summer reading clubs, moderate online book discussions, or create MySpace groups for specific books/authors. (Unfortunately, 79% had not used them in this manner.)

- 52% had used social networking sites for programming linked to technology, such as teaching teens how to share videos and pictures, training them how to develop MySpace pages or how to set up blogs, or hosting online gaming nights (Lupa 2009, 105–6).

What are some of the barriers or issues encountered by librarians in using social networks with teens?

- Some librarians reported issues related to access to social networking sites. Initially their libraries blocked them owing to potential problems, but many had since provided access for their teens on library computers.
- Others reported that training programs for parents and community members were not well attended, but that teens seemed very aware of Internet safety and privacy issues.
- Librarians also reported negative experiences such as gang activity, cyberbullying, posting of X-rated material, and other disruptive behaviors (Lupa 2009, 103–4).

The Lupa findings provide a picture of librarians' impressions of why teens use social networking sites. They also give us some good examples of how these sites are being used and of positive and negative issues associated with their use. We can learn much from this study, but we should not interpret these findings as representative of all libraries or all librarians, keeping in mind that only a select group of librarians responded to the survey.

Study 2

The second study is our own 2009 analysis of public library websites and social networking pages (Abbas and Agosto 2009). We took a different approach to determine how many public libraries are using social networks with teens and how they are using them. Using a selection of libraries derived from Hennen's American Public Library Ratings (Hennen 2008) framework, we were able to put together a sample of public libraries serving a range of different populations.

We then examined the websites of the top 10 libraries in each of Hennen's 10 population categories, ranging from a service population of more than 500,000 to one of fewer than 1,000. We reviewed the library websites for references to library pages on any social networking sites. We also searched MySpace and Facebook to see if libraries that did not mention social networking on their websites nonetheless had pages on either of these sites, as they were the two largest social networks in existence at the time of the study. Our findings gave us a snapshot view of how a range of public libraries are using social networks with teens and also provided examples of specific technologies and services being offered.

Some of our findings are outlined below.

How many public libraries have social networking pages like MySpace or Facebook?

- 73% of the libraries serving populations over 100,000 had at least one page on either MySpace or Facebook, with neither MySpace nor Facebook as the dominant choice.

- 100% of the libraries in the largest service categories (those serving populations greater than 100,000) had library websites, and 93% had teen library websites or web pages specifically for teens. However, the majority did not have links from their library websites to their social networking pages.

- 75% of the mid-sized public libraries reviewed (those serving populations in the 25,000 and 50,000 ranges) had a page on MySpace or Facebook.

- 30% of smaller public libraries reviewed (those in the 5,000 and 10,000 population categories) had a library page on either MySpace or Facebook.

- For the smallest public libraries (those serving populations under 5,000), just 8% used social networks to provide library services (Abbas and Agosto 2010, 73–74).

In other words, the larger the population served, the more likely the library was to have either a MySpace or Facebook page.

What social networking technologies and tools are present on public library websites and how are they being used with teens?

(For the purpose of this analysis, the smallest population categories of 2,500, 1,000, and under 1,000 were omitted, as none of these libraries had pages on social networking sites.)

- The most prevalent features included the following:
  - Links to library web pages
  - Photos of the libraries and of activities that took place there
  - Video clips of the libraries and library programs

- Links to other websites of interest to library patrons
- Blogs maintained by library staff
- Announcements of current events being held at the library (Abbas and Agosto 2010, 76)

- Of the libraries serving more than 100,000, more than half linked the library website to social networking pages, indicating a fairly strong linkage between the two types of online systems.
- Across all population categories, only 30% had dedicated teen pages within social networks.
- Across all population categories, 30% included descriptions of library services on their pages, and 56% included library photos.
- More than half of the libraries in the largest two categories included video clips on their pages. Less than half of those serving 100,000 or fewer included videos.
- About half of the libraries included external links on their pages to other websites of interest to teens.
- Generally, the larger the population served, the more likely it was that a blog would be included on the library website.
- Surprisingly, photos of book covers and reviews of new books were rare across nearly all of the size categories, indicating that few of these libraries are using their social networking pages to promote traditional book circulation (Abbas and Agosto 2010, 72–76).

It appears from this analysis that U.S. public libraries in all population categories provide many different features and services via social networks, but they do not necessarily focus on teens as their main user group. Moreover, features that libraries have chosen to include on their library websites and social networking pages do not necessarily reflect findings such as those of the Pew study reviewed earlier in this chapter. For example, many of the libraries included blogs on their websites. The 2010 Pew study found that teens are using blogs less, *50% less*, than suggested by equivalent figures from their 2006 study (Lenhart et al. 2010). If teens are losing interest in blogging, it doesn't make much sense to devote limited library resources and staff time to maintaining a library blog for teens. The same is true of any other online services or programs. Even if a company provides free access to the platform that hosts the program or service, library staff still need to devote precious time to updating and monitoring it. Librarians must remain aware of teens' changing online behaviors and update their online services accordingly, focusing their resources and efforts on the programs and services most likely to engage teens' interest.

HOW PUBLIC LIBRARIES USE SOCIAL NETWORKS TO SERVE TEENS: PUBLIC LIBRARY PROFILES

Another approach we can use to learn how public libraries are using social networks to connect with teens is to take a closer look at the kinds of technologies and services that a few libraries are using. Five public libraries that do use social networks to serve teens were chosen at random from U.S. public libraries listed on the lib-web-cats directory of public libraries in the United States (Breeding 2010). Each of these libraries is profiled below, in order from largest to smallest population served.

Profile 1: The Denver Public Library

The Denver Public Library serves a population of 568,913. It has one central library, 22 branches, and a bookmobile (National Center for Education Statistics 2007). At the time of our examination, the Denver Public Library's website included many social networking technologies and featured them prominently. There were links to MySpace, Facebook, Twitter, YouTube, Flickr, and Vimeo on the library's home page. Many of the library's social networking pages were not specifically focused on teens, but they did have MySpace, Twitter, and Flickr pages specifically for teens. All of the library's social networking pages had been updated very recently, and they appeared to be active. They had been "friended" or "liked" by teens, other public libraries, and authors who write for teens. The MySpace page was maintained by a teen.

The library's teen website was designed to catch teens' attention and keep it. The trendy design, customizable colors ("We chose mustard!"), many Web 2.0 features, and category labels were all geared to teens. For example, mousing over the category labeled "homework" revealed the following description: "The closest to cheating you can get without the guilt." Mousing over the "ask a librarian" category brought up the message: "Librarians DO know everything. Ask a question 24/7, get an answer fast!"

The library's teen website also included links to teen blogs, the teen MySpace page, homework help and database pages, author sites, book lists, the teen book of the day, movies, anime, and more. The most impressive

Web 2.0 feature was a space where teens could write reviews of books, movies, music, and other resources. Also of particular note was the "Life" link, described as "topics that you give a #$@* about!" It provided links to topics of interest to teens, such as "body," "mind," "future," "spirituality," and "sexuality."

While this library was actively using a wide variety of social networks, it was difficult to find the social networking pages targeted to teens. There were links at the bottom of the library's home page to each of the social networks in use but just to the general library pages, not the teen pages. Even the library's teen web page did not link to the MySpace or Flickr teen pages. The social networking pages did, however, link back to the main library's web page.

Profile 2: The Loudoun County Public Library

The Loudoun County Public Library, located in Loudoun County, Virginia, has a service population of 223,800. It serves the county with seven branches and one bookmobile (National Center for Education Statistics 2007). Its website included links to the teen library web page but no links to social networking sites. The library did, however, have a page on Facebook geared to all users, with content that was very heavily teen-oriented. Patrons would have to search Facebook to find it, since there was no link on the library's home page.

The library appeared to have a number of technology-based programs and services for teens. The "Just for Teens" page on the library's website included Web 2.0 features such as links to a teen blog, videos by teens and of teen programs, winners' entries in a short-story contest, photos, and announcements of contests and other teen programs. However, there were no links from the teen library's web page to the Facebook page, again making it difficult for potential users to find. Both the teen blog and the library's Facebook page appeared to be active and up to date. The Facebook page had been "friended" or "liked" by teens, other public libraries, and authors who write for teens.

Profile 3: The North Canton Public Library

The North Canton Public Library, located in North Canton, Ohio, serves a population of 28,076 and has just one main library with no branches (National Center for Education Statistics 2007). The library's home page included links to Twitter and Facebook, though these were to pages for general use, not to pages just for teens. The links were hard to see on the library home page, thus reducing their effectiveness in attracting patrons. Both the Facebook and Twitter pages contained current postings of library events and programs and appeared to be active.

The library's website also included a very teen-oriented teen web page called the Teen Circuit. It provided links to the teen advisory board, Anime/ Manga club, book lists and author sites, programming and pictures of past programs, and the library's teen blog (which unfortunately appeared to be inactive, as was a link to resource reviews). While this library seemed to be doing a good job of maintaining the teen library web page, it seemed to be missing out on reaching teens via social networks, perhaps in part because it is so much smaller than the first two libraries profiled here.

Profile 4: The Mitchell Public Library

Serving an even smaller population, the Mitchell Public Library is located in Mitchell, South Dakota. It serves 14,558 people with its single library building (National Center for Education Statistics 2007). It offered links from its main library web page to its MySpace page, and it also gave patrons the option of subscribing to news updates through RSS feeds (RSS, or Really Simple Syndication, feeds provide links to items of interest on the Internet as well as brief content summaries). The Mitchell Public Library RSS feeds included reports of library events, services, and announcements. The library's MySpace page was not geared specifically for teens but instead featured the life story and memorial to Festus, the library's turtle.

The teen library web page included links to LibraryThing, Shelfari, author sites, and fan fiction sites but no separate MySpace or Facebook pages. Several of the features on the teen library web page were designed to entice teens to participate in this online community. For example, the library's teen web page had Web 2.0 features that enabled teens to post their graphic novels and upload teen video book talks. The various pages were all up to date and contained recent postings.

Profile 5: The New Cumberland Public Library

Located in New Cumberland, Pennsylvania, the New Cumberland Public Library serves the smallest population of the five libraries profiled here. It is part of the Cumberland County Library System, which has eight libraries in different locations around the county. The New Cumberland location serves a population of just 7,349 people with its single library building (National Center for Education Statistics 2007). The library website is part of the county library system's website. It included links to several social networks, including Facebook, Blogger, Delicious, Flickr, and YouTube. The libraries in the system each maintained their own Facebook pages. All of various social networking pages were for general use, with no pages dedicated just to teen services.

In addition to this wealth of social networking tools, the county library system's teen web page contained links to their *very* active teen blog, teen advisory board, events, pictures, and surveys for teens. All of the sites contained up-to-date, useful posts and comments from patrons. County librarians were active in maintaining the book recommendations and other links on the Blogger and Delicious sites. The Delicious site included "Librarian's tagged websites"; the YouTube and Flickr sites both contained current pictures and videos of library events and programs. Considering the small size of the population served by this library, the wealth of systemwide online tools and services available to teens demonstrates the advantage for small libraries of participating in consortia and other resource-sharing systems.

These five library profiles show us how a random set of public libraries is making use of social networks and other Web 2.0 features in some innovative and teen-oriented ways, although at this point the percentage of public libraries nationally that offer these services is unclear. Many of the social networking technologies described throughout this book are in use at these five libraries, such as fan fiction and author sites; social bookmarking/social cataloging sites like Delicious, LibraryThing, Shelfari, and Goodreads; blogs and microblogs like Twitter; and photo- and video-sharing sites like Flickr and YouTube.

As a group, these five libraries are working to integrate social networks into their teen services, but they are doing so with mixed success. Creating social network pages and profiles and linking them to the library's website is just the first step in integration. Active maintenance and staff participation is the next step for the effective use of these tools. Most of these libraries had successfully created social network pages and profiles, but their success in maintaining and updating them varied from frequent maintenance and participation to near abandonment.

WHERE DO WE GO FROM HERE?

Beyond understanding the specific kinds of services offered, we need to learn more about *why* libraries choose the social networking technologies they do and the factors that affect their choices. The reasons why these five libraries chose these features and particular social networks cannot be determined from this analysis. Some factors might, for example, involve the time and staff needed to develop and maintain sites and features, technical skills or availability of technical support, and administrative support for time to develop and update sites and also to train staff how to use the necessary technologies. We also need to hear more success stories (and perhaps stories where these technologies did not work as planned) to help more librarians decide the best paths for moving their teen services into the social networking arena.

Until more research becomes available, a good place online to track developments and links to libraries that are using social networks and other Web 2.0/Library 2.0 tools is "Library Success: A Best Practices Wiki," developed by Meredith Farkas. It includes successful (and sometimes unsuccessful) stories about libraries' use of technologies, programming ideas, and services for different populations. Of particular relevance to this chapter are the following collections of links: "Libraries using Social Networks," "Teens and MySpace," and "Teens and Blogs." Because this is a wiki, librarians can become members at no cost and share their experiences and links to their library pages with others in the library community.

What is also evident from these five profiles and from the two studies discussed above is that while the professional literature is replete with great ideas and examples of how to use social networking technologies effectively (e.g., Chu and Meulemans 2008; Evans 2006; Harris 2006; and Miller and Jensen 2007), it appears that these ideas have been slow to carry over into practice. More importantly, libraries' choices of social networking technologies may not be based on our best resource of all, *the teens themselves*, and on the social networking technologies that they would like to use. We need to make teens' preferences a driving force in the design and delivery of library services. Chapter 2 describes how teens use these tools and how libraries can work to make library programs and services better match teens' social networking behaviors and preferences.

REFERENCES

Abbas, June, and Denise E. Agosto. "Urban Teens and Online Social Networking." In *The Information Needs and Behaviors of Urban Teens: Research and Practice,* edited by D. E. Agosto and S. Hughes-Hassell, 67–82. Chicago: ALA Editions, 2010.

Agosto, Denise E., and June Abbas. "Teens and Social Networking: How Public Libraries Are Responding to the Latest Online Trend." *Public Libraries* 48 (2009): 32–37.

Breeding, Marshall. "Public Libraries in the United States." 2010, http://www. librarytechnology.org/USPublicLibraries.pl?SID=20100729534088134& code=lwca (accessed July 5, 2010).

Chu, Melanie, and Yvonne Nalani Meulemans. "The Problems and Potential of MySpace and Facebook Usage in Academic Libraries." *Internet Reference Services Quarterly* 13, no. 1 (Spring 2008): 69–85.

Evans, Beth. "Your Space or MySpace." *LJ NetConnect* (Fall 2006): 8–10, 12.

Harris, Christopher. "MySpace Can be Our Space: Let's Turn the Infamous Networking Site into a Teachable Moment." *School Library Journal* 52, no. 5 (May 2006): 30.

Hennen, Thomas J. "Hennen's American Public Library Ratings 2008." *American Libraries* 39, no. 9 (October 2008): 56–61, http://www.haplr-index.com/ HAPLR08_CorrectedVersionOctober8_2008.pdf/ (accessed May 10, 2010).

Lenhart, Amanda, Kristen Purcell, Aaron Smith, and Kathryn Zickuhr. "Social Media and Young Adults." Washington, DC: Pew Internet & American Life Project, February 3, 2010, http://pewinternet.org/Reports/2010/Social-Media-and-Young-Adults.aspx (accessed July 5, 2010).

Lupa, Robyn M. "A National View—Survey and a Challenge." In *More than MySpace: Teens, Librarians, and Social Networking*, edited by Robyn M. Lupa, 99–107. Santa Barbara, CA: Libraries Unlimited, 2009.

Miller, Sarah Elizabeth, and Lauren A. Jensen. "Connecting and Communicating with Students on Facebook." *Computers in Libraries* 27, no. 8 (September 2007): 18–22.

National Center for Education Statistics. "Public Libraries Survey, Fiscal Year 2005," http://nces.ed.gov/pubsearch/pubsinfo.asp?pubid=2008301 (accessed July 22, 2010).

WEBSITES

Denver Public Library, http://denverlibrary.org/

Farkas, Meredith. Library Success: A Best Practices Wiki, http://libsuccess.org/ index.php?title=Main_Page/

Loudon County Public Library, http://library.loudoun.gov/

Loudon County Public Library teen web page, http://library.loudoun.gov/ Default.aspx?tabid=286/

Mitchell Public Library, http://mitlib.sdln.net/

Mitchell Public Library teen web page, http://mitlib.sdln.net/teen_programs/ teens.html/

New Cumberland Public Library, http://www.cumberlandcountylibraries.org/ index.aspx?nid=90/

New Cumberland Public Library teen web page, http://www.cumberlandcounty libraries.org/index.aspx?NID=266/

North Canton Public Library, http://www.ncantonlibrary.org/

North Canton Public Library teen web page, http://www.ncantonlibrary.org/ Teen/default.htm/

2

◇ ◇ ◇

LOOKING CLOSELY AT TEENS' USE OF SOCIAL NETWORKS: WHAT DO HIGH SCHOOL SENIORS DO ONLINE?

Denise E. Agosto, Joyce Kasman Valenza, and June Abbas

In order to use social networks for the effective delivery of library services and instruction to teens, we first need to understand how teens use these tools in their everyday lives. With this goal in mind, we set out to study how students attending a highly technological high school use social networks and other information and communication technologies (ICTs) for personal communication purposes. This chapter describes the study and the results. It also explains what the results indicate for the successful delivery of public and school library services to teens.

DESCRIBING THE STUDY

We chose to use focus group interviews to conduct this study. A focus group is an interview in which one or two moderators question a group of people at the same time. Typically there are about six to ten participants in each focus group session. The moderators usually run a series of focus groups, stopping when no new information is coming to light. The moderators work from a predetermined interview guide (a list of questions) with each group, and they are careful to give each focus group participant the chance to answer each of these questions. The goal of the focus group technique is to determine people's thoughts and opinions on issues of interest, such as opinions on a new product or reactions to a newly proposed law, making it a good choice for investigating student attitudes about social networks.

THE STUDY PARTICIPANTS

We held a series of six focus group interviews with a total of 45 students in the senior class of the selected high school. There were 34 boys and 11 girls in the six interview sessions (see Table 2.1 for details).

In a qualitative study such as this, it's important to understand the context of the research and the perspectives of the research participants. The high school where this study took place is located on the outskirts of a large eastern U.S. city. It serves a primarily white middle- to upper-middle-class population. As of September 2009, there were 775 students enrolled in grades eight through twelve. Slightly over 90% of its 2009 graduates continued on to some form of higher education. For the academic year 2009–2010, there were 162 students in the senior class.

The school district places great emphasis on the delivery of education via digital technologies. Within the district there are interactive whiteboards in every classroom in grades 5 to 12 and digital projectors in all K–12 classrooms. In addition to traditional computer labs in each school and each school library, there are 18 mobile computer labs in the high school, 6 in the middle school, and 4 in the elementary schools. Beginning in the 2010–2011 school year, completion of a computer science course will be a high school graduation requirement for all incoming ninth-grade students. The school is also listed among the Classrooms for the Future

Table 2.1: Focus Group Participants

Group	Males	Females	Total
Group 1	3	7	10
Group 2	6	1	7
Group 3	10	1	11
Group 4	4	1	5
Group 5	5	1	6
Group 6	6	0	6
Total	**34**	**11**	**45**

recipient, a program that equips high school English, math, science, and social studies classrooms in participating schools with enhanced technology and provides Internet-connected laptop computers for every teacher and every student.

All this is to say that these teens came from mostly middle-class white backgrounds and that they had received considerable technology exposure and instruction in school. As a result, it is likely that they were more active users of social networks and other technologies than the average U.S. teenager. This makes them ideal targets for providing library services via social networks. We can also look to them for teen technology leaders and study their thoughts and behaviors as a basis for thinking about the future of electronic library services to teens.

The focus group sessions were conducted in a private meeting room inside the high school. For each session, one moderator and one note taker was present, and the sessions were audiotaped. Each session lasted approximately one to one-and-a-half hours. The focus group guide included questions related to the students' preferred technologies for communicating with friends and family and why they preferred those technologies, the reasons why they did or did not engage in online social networking, how they selected tools for social networking and other communication purposes, and how they decided whom to accept as online "friends."

After the focus group interviews were over, we analyzed the data using standard content analysis methods for qualitative data. The results of the data analysis are presented and explained in the next sections of this chapter.

WHAT DID WE LEARN ABOUT TEENS AND THEIR USE OF SOCIAL NETWORKS?

The first thing we learned is that when we're talking about teens, it's impossible to separate social networks from other methods of mediated communication, such as texting and talking via cell phones. These teens thought more in terms of the end goal—communication—than the specific technologies they would use to reach that goal. Thus, although we had intended to focus only on social network use, we ended up studying teens' use of other information and communication technologies (ICTs) as well, particularly their use of cell phones.

In general, these students tended to view social networks and cell phones from a pragmatic standpoint. They saw them as tools for quick and easy communication and as useful for relationship building and maintenance, more than as high-tech toys or gadgets. The students selected their communication media based on the closeness of the relationship they had with the message receiver and on the number of intended receivers. Texting via cell phones was the most frequent means of mediated communication, occurring throughout the day at school, home, work, and social events. Most sent frequent text messages—often many times each day—to communicate with a select group of about four to six close friends, including boyfriends and girlfriends, and many also texted and called their parents and other relatives, although less frequently.

Interestingly, although nearly all of the students were frequent cell phone users, most voiced hesitation about using traditional landline telephones. As one of the girls said, "I don't answer the [home] phone anymore." Much of this reluctance came from privacy concerns and from a general distrust of landline telephones. The teens agreed that nearly everyone they would want to talk to on the telephone had their cell phone numbers, meaning that landline callers were mostly telemarketers, callers dialing wrong numbers, and other strangers with whom they did not want to interact.

Teens' Social Networking and ICT Use Patterns

In terms of online social networking, these students tended to use social networks—Facebook in particular—for less frequent contact with a much wider range of friends and sometimes parents, siblings, and other relatives. Roughly half of the students in the study used social networks daily; slightly fewer used them a few times a week; and three of the students did not use online social networks at all. Facebook was the social network of choice for nearly all of the students who used social networks. Just 1 of the 45 students was an avid user of MySpace. A few other students indicated that they did not have active MySpace accounts but that they did use MySpace for listening to music.

Common social network activities included posting photos for distribution and archival purposes, broadcasting information about social gatherings and sports events, gathering information about new friends and casual acquaintances, and making contact with lost friends and physically distant acquaintances. Librarians interested in using social networks to connect with teens can design services to meet these uses, such as using library social network pages to post pictures from library programs, advertise upcoming programs and events, announce new homework and other course-related resources, and try to attract new library users.

On the whole, these teens tended to use social technologies differently for communication with adults than with peers. A minority had friended their parents on Facebook. Most, however, scoffed at the idea. As one of the teens explained: "It adds another layer of connectivity that you don't need." When asked if they would friend a teacher on Facebook, the prevailing opinion was no. "It's creepy," said one student with a grimace. It is therefore unlikely that large numbers of teens would want to friend their librarians. They are more likely to turn to library pages on social networks as informational sources rather than turning to librarians as online friends for purposes of personal or school-related communication.

Although texting and Facebook dominated the teens' communication with friends, they tended to prefer e-mail for interactions with teachers because it's "less personal." With e-mail, "they can't see your profile." Therefore librarians should not abandon e-mail contact with teens in favor of social networks but rather use both contact methods for maximizing the ways in which teens can choose to communicate with their libraries and librarians.

As a group, these students were heavy users of ICTs. Many of them echoed the sentiments that "texting is pretty addicting," and that "I use Facebook pretty much all of the time." One of the boys said that his most recent phone bill indicated that he had sent over 1,000 text messages the previous month. One of the girls in another session said that she had sent over 1,500 text messages the previous month. Others in these sessions chimed in to say that their use of texting was about as frequent, sending an average of about 30 to 35 text messages per day. These numbers might seem high, but they are consistent with recent data on teen cell phone use (Lenhart et al. 2010). Regardless of the exact numbers, these students considered themselves to be very frequent users of text messaging and of Facebook, often referring to themselves as "addicted" to technology.

How Do Teens Select Social Networks and Other ICTs?

Just as important as understanding which technologies teens prefer to use for communication and information purposes is understanding *why* they prefer them. Overall, we learned from this study that for teens, there is no one preferred method for mediated communication. Instead, teens select the technologies that they will use to contact people based on a number of contextual factors, most notably the relationship with the intended message recipients and with the number of intended recipients, as discussed above, as well as based on simplicity of use, speed of communication, the ability to maintain constant contact, and multitasking capabilities.

Simplicity of Use

Head and Eisenberg (2010) found that one of the main reasons undergraduates choose to use *Wikipedia* for academic research was the simplicity of its interface. For the participants in the current study, the overwhelming social network of choice was Facebook, and the simplicity of its interface was one of its main attractions, both for students who considered themselves to be heavy technology users and for those who were more reluctant users. For example, one of the girls explained that:

> Technology is not my thing. Facebook, they kind of set it up so it's easy to get your way around it. Like with MySpace, I haven't used it because it is so complicated. And I don't even know what Twitter is. But Facebook seems like the easiest to use out of all of them [so I use it].

One of the boys explained why he had switched from using MySpace to using Facebook:

> At the start it [MySpace] was okay, but it became really annoying. The only reason I would be on MySpace would be to communicate with someone, and I would click on their profile, and they would have so much garbage on their site, music playing. It got to be way too much. MySpace was not as simple [as Facebook].

This quote shows how teens tend to view social networks more as communication tools than as entertainment resources.

Of the 45 students, only 3 (all boys) lacked active Facebook profiles. When asked why they did not use Facebook or other social networking utilities, one of the boys replied: "I think if I actually had a Facebook [page] I would be too lazy to go on and check it and write stuff. If I want to talk to someone, I would rather call them up or text them. I think it is easier."

When asked why texting was so popular, again simplicity of use was a determining factor. The heavy texters all agreed that they texted so often because texting is "simple and fast." On the other hand, those who were less frequent texters found its physical and cognitive requirements to be taxing. As one of the boys explained: "I am not a fan of texting. I am not that coordinated. My phone has small buttons."

The lesson to be learned here is that simplicity is key to providing electronic library services for teens. Librarians should make sure that their online services are easy for teens to use and that their social network pages are not overly cluttered or overwhelming to navigate.

Speed of Communication

Related to the idea of simplicity of use was a preference for social networks and other technologies that could be used quickly and that enabled immediate responses from the intended message recipients. Students in all six sessions agreed that they were texting much more frequently than in the past and that texting had largely replaced talking on telephones, both cell phones and landlines. When asked why, there was widespread agreement that texting is a much faster form of communication: "It takes two seconds" to send a text message. Even though text messaging conversations could last over a period of days, each conversational turn was seen as quick and efficient and therefore the best choice for frequent, brief communication: "Text messaging is good for short, quick things."

Not all of the students agreed that texting was quick and easy. One of the boys who considered himself to be an infrequent texter explained that: "I think it is just easier to call someone and say what needs to be said rather than [typing] a whole big spill of text." Another boy complained that "text messages can go on for days," since, unlike face-to-face or telephone conversations, there are fewer physical constraints that necessitate ending a conversation.

For most of the participants, however, text messaging was the first choice for contacting close friends because of the speed and simplicity of sending and receiving messages. As one of the girls explained: "Normally everyone else has their phones right by them, so you can get an answer back right away."

This preference for quick communication means that librarians should be careful to make library contact information easy to find on all library pages and that they should try to provide quick responses to electronic requests for help. It also means that teens are unlikely to spend time searching for links to social network pages and to other online services if they are hidden a few clicks beyond the library's homepage. Visibility and speed of access are key for engaging teens' interest and participation.

Constant Contact

Frand (2000) has suggested that for today's young adults, "constant connectivity—being in touch with friends and family at any time and from any place—is of utmost importance" (p. 15). Especially in the case of texting with close friends, the students in this study wanted to be able to carry on conversations and other mediated interactions, as one student said, "any place, at any time." Most of the students had at least one tool for mediated communication within easy reach at all times. One of the boys described his daily use of Facebook as lasting for hours: "Right when I get home, I just log onto Facebook and leave it on in the background for the rest of the night. And when I am out doing other things, I am texting or calling people."

Another one of the boys explained his frequent electronic communication patterns with his girlfriend and closest friends as varying in frequency yet occurring on a nearly daily basis:

> I am always connected to my girlfriend...I have a group of friends that text me or call me on a regular basis, and out of them it might be one in a day or a couple of them [who text or call me each day]. Some days are higher than others.

The nearly universal ownership of cell phones enabled this high rate of electronic communication, making cell phones virtually constant presences in these students' lives. Nearly all of them carried cell phones to school, to work, and to social events, making them "always connected" to their close friends. As one of the boys explained:

> I got an iphone, and I got a Facebook application on my iphone. I have had it for almost a month, and it has never left my body. It has been in my pocket or next to my bed...never more than three feet away.

It's important to note that the students who could access Facebook via cell phones were much more avid users of social networks than those who were limited to computer access. Discussing his preference for texting over social networking, one of the boys explained that "Facebook has a lot more information, but you have to be at a computer to use it. So it is not really mobile." This means that libraries need to be aware that students from more advantaged backgrounds—those more likely to have high-capability cell phones—are more likely to be heavy social network users than those from less advantaged backgrounds, simply due to access issues. This is an important consideration in designing library services to be delivered via social networks. Librarians must be careful to provide the same services via alternate technologies so that teens with access limitations can participate on an equal level as those with ready access.

Multitasking

A common theme that runs through the discussions of the online communication habits of today's teens is their heavy use of multitasking (see, for example, Brown 2000; Foehr 2006; Frand 2000; and Wallis 2006). For most of the teens in this study, multitasking was indeed a habitual behavior, and they preferred ICTs that could support their multitasking habits. For example, one of the boys explained that his most typical online activities included listening to music, checking Facebook, checking online sports scores, watching videos on YouTube, texting, playing games, doing homework, and e-mailing—usually all at once. Most of the students agreed that they multitasked while doing homework in particular: "Last night I was on the library [website] here, and I had Twitter open. I also had my Gmail open, *NY Times*, and Microsoft Word open, and I still did my [school] project in half an hour."

Another reason for the popularity of texting was that it lent itself especially well to multitasking. As one of the boys explained: "You can almost do anything that doesn't require two hands and text at the same time." Most of the participants agreed that texting while in the presence of others was so common that "In most cases I won't notice." On the other hand, they disapproved if the texter became too distracted to participate in the face-to-face conversation:

> It can be annoying....I was driving in a car with a friend of mine and she was texting, but she couldn't keep the conversation going with me and text at the same time without stopping. So there were breaks in our conversation. But if you can text and keep a conversation fluid, I don't see a problem with that.

When asked why they chose to multitask, there was general agreement that multitasking relieved boredom: "I know that I have gotten so used to a high-paced lifestyle that I am uncomfortable and uneasy when things slow down. If I am just at home with nothing to do, I am unsure what to do with myself."

As far as library services are concerned, librarians must realize that teens are likely to engage in multiple activities while taking part in online library services and programs. This means that rather than using a social network page to promote just one activity or information medium, such as just providing online reviews of new YA books or just creating a collaborative blog for teens, librarians should provide teens with a variety of online activity choices, including activities that can be undertaken simultaneously. For example, a library could use its Facebook page to provide links to popular music-sharing sites and to book recommendations and a teen collaborative blog.

WHAT DOES ALL OF THIS MEAN FOR LIBRARY SERVICES TO TEENS?

Now that we understand how teens are using social networks and other ICTs for communication and information purposes, the question becomes how best to harness these tools for the effective delivery of library services. From this study, we can learn at least four rules to guide the design of online library services for teens: (1) use multiple contact methods, (2) employ frequent updating and maintenance, (3) help teens stay connected by providing access, and (4) talk to teens to learn about their changing communication and information needs.

Lesson 1: Use Multiple Contact Methods

To date, most libraries have focused on the library website as the one main tool for the delivery of online library services to teens. Our study shows that teens use an array of social networks and ICTs and that, for most teens, library websites are not among the most frequently used of these tools. To gain the attention of teens who are often online but who are not as often on the library's website, librarians should use multiple online tools to promote their services and collections as well as providing links to connect the library's various online programs and services to each other.

Further, this study indicates that teens are often uncomfortable friending adults such as teachers and librarians. Many teens are, however, willing to join library pages on Facebook and other social networks. This makes organizational social network pages good tools for providing basic library contact information, upcoming program announcements, blurbs promoting new book and media acquisitions, contact points for homework assistance, and more. Of course, for teens who do use library websites or for those looking to connect to the library via social networks, there should be clearly labeled, prominent links between the library website and all social network pages to facilitate easy access.

On the other hand, just promoting the library via the library website and one or more social networks ignores the fact that for many teens, the most constant IT presence in their lives is the cell phone, and their preferred method of cell phone communication is text messaging. Since cell phone texting is typically limited to communicating with a small group of intimate friends and sometimes close family members, teens are unlikely to want to send or receive frequent generic texts to and from librarians. Instead, librarians can use cell phone texting and even talking on cell phones to provide more specialized library services to teens, such as reference and research assistance, which are less frequent and more intimate interactions than program promotion and public relations efforts.

In addition, young people's growing reliance on mobile devices as information sources points to the value of creating applications for those devices. Catalog and database applications, as well as access to student resources, should be available to young people interested in accessing them via their cell phones. In view of teens' heavy use of texting via cell phones, text-a-librarian services might become increasingly popular as well.

Lesson 2: Employ Frequent Updating and Maintenance

The use of these multiple technologies to reach teens can remain effective only if librarians are willing to be flexible and to change their service delivery modes as teens' ICT uses and preferences change. For example, a couple of years ago the majority of the teens in this study were avid MySpace users. In just a few short years, nearly all of them abandoned MySpace in favor of Facebook. If a library had been providing services to them via MySpace, the power of MySpace for reaching them would likely have diminished greatly with the onset of Facebook dominance. And while Twitter had not gained popular ground at the time our focus groups were held, it is possible that more students would be tweeting and following Twitter feeds if we interviewed them again now. In order to remain effective, the library in this example would have had to migrate its services from MySpace to Facebook, and then it would have had to be prepared to move them again and again every few years or even more frequently as new social networks and even new technologies emerged and came to dominate teens' online use patterns.

In addition to periodically reevaluating which social networks and other ICTs are best for reaching teens, the content provided via these tools must be kept up to date and visible. It's not enough just to create a library page on a social network, link it to the library website, and hope that it garners a lot of teen followers. When most of the teens in this study were asked, they couldn't remember how many organizations and causes they had joined via social networks or even which ones they had joined. If libraries just enable teens to identify as fans or friends of their pages and then do little else, teens will likely forget about them. If librarians want to stay in teens' minds, they must frequently update their social network pages and announce the updates to users. Posting notices of new photos from successful teen programs and announcements of forthcoming events, for example, can remind teens that the library is there for them to use, both online and in person. It's a simple marketing rule that people use a service more frequently if they are reminded on a regular basis that it exists. The same is true of communicating with teachers and other adult collaborators about the library's electronic services. Frequent messages are necessary to stay in potential collaborators' minds and to remind them of the ongoing value of collaboration.

Lesson 3: Help Teens Stay Connected by Providing Access

This study also shows us how important it is for most teens to maintain constant electronic contact with their close friends, and sometimes with their family members as well. While it is unlikely that most teens would want to remain in constant contact with their public or school librarians, this does mean that an important ongoing role for libraries is enabling teens to remain connected to the people in their own personal social networks. Particularly for teens who lack easy access to social networks and other ICTs, libraries can help teens stay connected to the online social world by providing access to popular social networks and other forms of social media, such as YouTube and other digital content-sharing sites. Unfortunately, many public and school libraries block access to these tools, thinking that they promote the wasting of time instead of realizing that they can help teens learn developmentally beneficial communication and information practices. We can use these online spaces to celebrate young people's creative content—their digital stories, art work, book reviews, discussions, and trailers, etc.—and to offer them places for healthy self-expression.

Librarians can help to lift these access barriers in public libraries or school library media centers by developing programs and forming collaborations with teachers and/or school administrators and other library professionals with the goal of educating each other about the benefits of providing access to social networking sites. Librarians can also serve as advocates for teens by providing more information about the benefits of social networking to teens' communities (parents, teachers, and other key players in teens' everyday life experiences).

Lesson 4: Talk to Teens to Learn about Their Changing Communication and Information Needs

For these teens, Facebook and texting via cell phones were the clear communication modes of choice, but these top choices will likely change in a few years, and then change again and again as communication and information technologies continue to evolve. As one of the boys said: "They'll always keep making new technologies to keep us in touch with each other." As a result, the importance of involving teens in the design of electronic library services cannot be overstated. The real experts on teens' thoughts and behaviors are teens themselves, and the best way to keep library services relevant to teens' evolving interests and behaviors is to create formal and informal avenues for the ongoing collection of teen input. These avenues can include teen advisory boards, teen idea and design teams, periodic surveys, informal focus groups, volunteering and internship opportunities, and other informal conversations with teens.

Also of importance is for librarians to keep their knowledge and skills up to date when it comes to learning about the latest social networks and other technologies popular with teens. The best way to do this is to use these tools to learn more about their potential for reaching out to teens and providing library services to them. This means that librarians should set up their own MySpace or Facebook pages, or practice using the tools by creating library profiles and library pages within these networks. Librarians interested in keeping their technology skills up to date can also try different ways of communicating with teens to see what works best within their own library communities. Reading the professional literature and popular press reports about social networking tools and ICTs and attending professional development workshops at library and other professional conferences are also good ways to learn what new technologies are being developed and how they might be adopted by teens.

Last, librarians should become advocates for teens and social networking as a way to help parents, guardians, teachers, and other adults learn about the social and educational benefits of engaging in online social networking. Advocacy can take the form of writing about experiences and sharing successes *and lessons learned* through the development of professional and local programs. Good venues for sharing success stories include library blogs, professional journals, professional conferences, and library and school community listservs.

CONCLUSION

Above all, public and school librarians need to take their services and programs to where today's teens are, and today's teens are very often online in social networks or texting via cell phones. We are not challenging the ongoing importance of physical library buildings or of face-to-face library services. Libraries have been around in one form or another for many hundreds (even thousands!) of years, and we believe that they will continue to exist for many centuries to come. The format of our libraries, however, must change as user needs and behaviors evolve, and the same is true of our service delivery modes. Electronic library services to teens should complement but not replace face-to-face services, and librarians should consider how instruction and services can be offered as hybrids. Delivering library services to teens via social networks and other ICTs is one way librarians can ensure that future generations will continue to value and use their school and public libraries as teens' communication and information practices move increasingly into the online social world.

REFERENCES

Brown, John Seely. "Growing up Digital." *Change* 32 (2000): 10–20.

Foehr, Ulla G. "Media Multitasking among American Youth." Menlo Park, CA: Kaiser Family Foundation, 2006, http://www.kff.org/entmedia/upload/7592.pdf/ (accessed May 8, 2010).

Frand, Jason L. "The Information-Age Mindset." *EDUCAUSE Review* 35 (2000): 14–20.

Head, Alison J., and Michael B. Eisenberg. "How Today's College Students Use *Wikipedia* for Course-Related Research." *First Monday* 15 (March 1, 2010), http://firstmonday.org/htbin/cgiwrap/bin/ojs/index.php/fm/article/view/2830 (accessed May 8, 2010).

Lenhart, Amanda, Rich Ling, Scott Campbell, and Kristen Purcell. "Teens and Mobile Phones." Washington, DC: Pew Internet & American Life Project,

April 20, 2010, http://pewinternet.org/Reports/2010/Teens-and-Mobile-Phones.aspx (accessed May 1, 2010).

Wallis, Claudia. "The Multitasking Generation." *Time* 167 (2006): 48–55.

WEBSITES

Classrooms for the Future, http://www.portal.state.pa.us/portal/server.pt/community/classrooms_for_the_future/475/

3

◇ ◇ ◇

HOW SOCIAL NETWORKING SITES AID IN TEEN DEVELOPMENT

Sean Rapacki

Elsewhere in this book you'll see chapters about both the widespread popularity and the relative safety of social networking sites used by teens. But even if librarians come to terms with these aspects of online social networking, often there is still a nagging suspicion that such Internet activity is not particularly valuable or healthy beyond the entertainment it offers. After all, it's not like playing FarmVille on Facebook is going to prepare you for a career in agriculture. But MySpace and Facebook are more than just fun and games. Sites like these can aid teens in essential aspects of their development. This chapter examines how social networking sites can be socially and educationally useful to teen development and explores some of the ways libraries can encourage such activity.

WHAT DO TEENS NEED TO SUCCEED?

Before worrying about the technology, which is, after all, a means rather than an end, let's focus on teens and their needs. This may sound

This chapter is dedicated to Allen Nichols, who has given me a chance to serve as a teen librarian and has always offered me the encouragement and support to offer innovative services to our teen customers.

simplistic, but if you keep in mind that we're still discovering how the brains of young adults function and how they differ from the brains of adults, it makes sense not to assume automatically, from the start, that we know what teens need to support their healthy development into adulthood.

According to McElhaney, Anthonishak, and Allen (2008), a crucial predictor of teens' long-term ability to function socially is their own perception of their social success. In other words, if teens perceive themselves to be liked and to have friends, one can fairly reliably predict that their emotional development and social relations as adults will flourish. Interestingly enough, this study showed that what was of primary importance as a predictor of future success was not the reality of teens' relative popularity but their perception, however inaccurate, of it. Thus, teens need things that make them feel successful socially in order to legitimately achieve such goals as adults.

It's not all about potentially false perceptions, however. Lenhart (2009), a researcher with the Pew Internet and American Life Project, argues that while a minority of teens do adopt different personas online, what the majority of teens need and seek is a unified or integrated sense of identity, both online and in the real world (Wartella, Caplovitz, and Lee 2004). Sure, adolescence is a time when teens get to try on different types of identities; but what matters in the end is finding what is authentic for them. That doesn't mean that they can't change over time, just that they have a significant need for a sense of identity that feels stable and whole.

Emotional and social needs are only half the picture for successful teen development, however, particularly in these difficult economic times. Hall (2006) isn't overstating this case when she says that ignoring the integration of technological skill building in youth development risks nothing less than the opportunity for teens to develop meaningful and productive lives as adults. She further states that programs that accomplish this must be organic and draw from the real lives of young people.

What a teen needs to develop successfully, then, is a combination of the social and emotional (feeling that one has friends and an integrated sense of identity) as well as an array of technological skills that are an essential component of what the Partnership for 21st Century Skills promotes. To top it all off, each of these developmental goals must have roots in teens' own lives in order to feel authentic and be fully actualized. This sounds not only like a challenge that an army composed of well-meaning parents, teachers, and therapists might find difficult but one that might very well be impossible. After all, what self-respecting teen wouldn't respond as in the song "Run to the Hills," performed by Iron Maiden (Harris 1982), and "run to the hills" when faced with such an army of well-intentioned authority figures? I'm an adult, and I must admit the idea frightens even me a bit.

HOW DO SOCIAL NETWORKING SITES GIVE TEENS WHAT THEY NEED?

Luckily, nature abhors a vacuum. And by nature, of course, I mean the Internet. What could be more natural, after all, than this vast interactive information buffet for providing services that fulfill the needs of some of the huge teen demographic? In her presentation on the democratization of social networking sites, Lenhart (2009) states that 65% of teens aged 12 to 17 use sites like Facebook and MySpace. The reason for this high rate of use isn't merely the ubiquitous popularity of the online dice game Farkle or a burning desire to repeatedly watch trailers for *Twilight New Moon*. Social networking sites attract teens in droves because they help fulfill those very same vital developmental needs discussed above.

For instance, sites like Facebook and MySpace have turned the word *friend* into a verb, a sure sign that they help young people to feel that they are liked and have friends. The very idea that someone would want to view your photos, read your blogs, and comment on your profile page on such sites is based on the premise that people are interested in you. Game applications on these sites, like Mafia Wars and FarmVille, encourage you to recruit friends, pass on gifts, and become part of ever-expanding virtual communities. You can also suggest to your friends that they add one of your friends, thereby strengthening your network and reducing the degrees of separation. All in all, social networking sites seem to be constantly looking for new ways to promote the idea of "friending" as an active process in which all people can be successfully involved. Truly, if teens need to feel that they have friends and are liked, social networking sites seem tailor-made for fulfilling this need.

Who Am I? (Chan 1999) is more than a Jackie Chan movie; it's one of the ultimate questions we all must face, right up there with figuring out the meaning of life. And sometimes figuring out the meaning of life seems like the simpler of the two quests. At no time does the question of identity become more important and more challenging than for the young adult. After all, as the phrase *young adult* itself suggests, the adult identity embraced by teens is nascent and only partly developed at best. Becoming comfortable with who you are is like breaking in a new pair of shoes; it takes time and can sometimes be painful.

If you take a look at what teens actually do when they are online, as I have done with both my own teen stepchildren as well as with the many teen customers who friend our library, you'll find an amazing amount of time spent filling out surveys and quizzes. Who was the last person you spoke with on the phone? What makes you laugh? Is there someone you have a crush on? The answers to these and many other burning questions are posted daily on MySpace bulletins and Facebook walls by teens anxious not just to share who they are with others but also to confront that person themselves. If you type your answer and post it for the world to read, that makes it more true, something you can count on. One of the more popular crazes on Facebook is constructing quizzes for your friends to take to see how well they know you. Making such a quiz forces you to ask yourself what it is that defines you and what you want your friends to know about you. Whether they are taking or making surveys, teens are using social networking sites to find out who they are and to become more comfortable with those identities.

Quizzes are only a small portion of how social networking sites aid teens in forming an integrated sense of identity. Photo galleries let them display themselves in a variety of moods and poses, allowing teens to become comfortable with who they are on the outside. Page "pimping" features in MySpace that enable them to include personalized jukeboxes and backgrounds allow teens to express their inner landscapes. Both Facebook and MySpace encourage users to post their current mood or status, as an ever-changing thermometer of how they are doing. Of course social networking sites are not single software programs. They are bundles of applications, many of which are devoted to helping the user to answer that same challenging question faced by an amnesiac Jackie Chan.

What else, you may wonder, is that magical bundle of apps helping us to do while it is helping us to feel befriended and to figure out who we are? More than anything, social networking sites aid teens in becoming fluent in the use of technology in a way that is natural and integrated into their lives. Sites that aid you in pimping your profile let you choose style selections and then automatically create the HTML code for you to cut and paste into your profile settings, introducing the idea of the source code behind the Web and how it all works. Posting pictures or videos, at the very least, requires that you be able to navigate your computer to find the required files to upload. Games like FarmVille and Café World require participants to learn to schedule and manage their time, otherwise crops will die and food will get burnt. These and other games encourage collaborative online play, teach principles of economy and entrepreneurship, and, at their most basic level, encourage a spirit of enterprise, albeit in a virtual environment. Learning skills such as these and how to manage the bundle of apps that is a social networking site is precisely the type of natural learning process that can help young people attain the technological fluency they will need to survive in the 21st-century workplace and society. Thus, teens using social networking sites aren't just fulfilling emotional needs. They are integrating into their lives the technology and means of communication necessary for their success in the world of tomorrow.

Not only are there benefits for teens who use social networks, there are also benefits for the librarians who serve them. There is a tendency among adults, and I count myself among the guilty, to act as though time spent on social networking sites is time wasted rather than of value. And while sites like Facebook and MySpace are without a doubt fabulous places to waste time, there is something going on in the background that is anything but wasteful. Using such sites and incorporating them into your life makes you better prepared to assist teens who use them, not just with the technology but in interacting and collaborating with each other online.

WAYS LIBRARIES CAN USE SOCIAL NETWORKING SITES TO HELP PROMOTE HEALTHY TEEN DEVELOPMENT

I've tried to present evidence about some of what goes into the development of a successful teen, and I've further argued that those needs can be filled, to a significant extent, through use of social networking sites like Facebook and MySpace. I'm going to make a leap and assume that if you are reading a book of this nature, you're probably at least open to such possibilities. So, now what? How can libraries and librarians make use of this knowledge? What kinds of practices can teen librarians, in particular, adopt in order to encourage youth development and at the same time better engage teen customers to make the library more relevant in their lives? The short answer is that nobody really knows. This is new ground for all of us, and we won't really know until this generation of digital natives grows up whether our efforts have been truly successful and had a lasting impact. What I can share, however, are some of the ways in which I, as a librarian, have attempted to utilize the power of online social networking to reach teens.

The first thing I can suggest is creating a social network profile for either your library in general or for your teen department in particular. This may sound like a no-brainer, but there may be a lot of administrative and policy hurdles to clear before this becomes possible. One of the most basic policy questions you will have to address is who your library will accept as friends. Some libraries prefer to play it safe and friend only authors, librarians, and other libraries. After all, there is a legitimate concern about what it means to the reputation of your library when you are friends with customers who display questionable content on their profiles. By simply adopting a policy of not friending any customers, a library can avoid having to decide which customers are acceptable friends—a subjective process at best.

There are two problems with this safe approach. First, if you are not going to use friending as a way to become better engaged with your customers, it defeats the purpose of social networking sites. Second, adding your teen customers is one way to help fulfill their essential need to feel that they have friends. One way to resolve this dilemma is to accept that your library can no more control what customers do with their profiles than it can exclude members of the public from utilizing the library. The library is open to all who obey its regulations, and there is no reason its virtual presence should differ in this regard. Thus, as long as a customer doesn't include profanity in his or her screen name or nudity in the associated profile picture (things that wouldn't fly in the physical library either), he or she should not only be welcomed but also encouraged to join the library's social network. As a librarian, it makes me feel good to see at-risk youth hanging out in the library because I know there is at least a chance that they will discover our books and other resources. Engaging those same customers through an online presence is yet another way to increase their exposure to the opportunities that libraries afford.

Once teen customers become part of the library's online social network, there are many ways to engage them both socially and educationally. The enthusiastic response I get from teens after they have been friended by the library is a palpable example of how social networking sites can make the library more relevant to teen customers. That kind of sea change in how teens relate to the library would in itself be enough reason for using sites like MySpace and Facebook, but it is really just the beginning of the ways you can now interact with teen customers and engage them. Creating a profile and accepting friend requests from your teens captures their attention. The next challenge is to make sure you make the most of it.

One of the best ways to maximize the level of engagement your teen customers have with your online social networking presence is to actively seek their input. The whole concept of Web 2.0, and, by extension, Library 2.0, is aimed at making the user's experience an interactive rather than a passive one. It is precisely through these interactions that teens experience the social and educational support that they need for healthy development. As an example, let's take a look at some of the ways you can encourage interactivity through your library's MySpace or Facebook profile.

- First, there is the profile itself. If teen customers complain that your library's profile layout is too drab, you can give them the opportunity to help "pimp" it. Invite them to go to the profile layout design page of their choice, create a better-looking profile, and submit the HTML code generated by the site. You can then simply cut and paste the code into your profile editor to unleash your new teen-friendly profile. In what is truly a win–win situation, you get your library profile revamped and your teens develop their tech skills and feel like bigger stakeholders in their library.

- Blogs, bulletins, and comment sections all offer ways for your teens to interact and make their voices heard, although it is probably advisable to set your account so that all comments must be approved before being posted to public scrutiny. We have all heard about the research (National Institute of Mental Health 2001) showing that the logical portion of teen brains is not fully developed. There's no need to allow a momentary lapse of judgment on their part to do any mischief or to hurt either a teen's reputation or that of the library. Teens can use these methods of input to ask about programming, talk about books they like or want the library to acquire, comment on pictures of events posted by the library, or even embed their own homemade videos from YouTube as "commercials" for your teen advisory group or for other library activities.

- As you might expect, the ways in which teens themselves most often make use of social networking sites can give you ideas of the best ways to engage them and encourage their development. Does it seem as though the library's teen friends were constantly posting bulletins with the results of personality quizzes? If so, make sure that the library participates in some of that quiz action. Find out about the books they are reading; whether they prefer Bella, Harry Potter, or Naruto; and what their favorite thing about library programs is. Are your teens all about posting pics and vids on their profiles? Maybe you need to have an online photography or video contest. Let your teens be your guides.

As your teens interact with the library using means like these, they are fulfilling social needs, such as feeling that they have friends and developing a stable sense of identity. They are also developing a facility with technology that is among their most crucial educational needs for success in the 21st century (Hall 2006). While the use of social networking sites is far from a panacea for the needs of adolescence, it is easy to underestimate the importance of such activity in the lives of many young adults.

CONCLUSION

If the last couple of years have taught us anything, it is that an increasing use of technology doesn't have to lead to the depersonalization of library service. The social interaction of Web 2.0 provides an opportunity to get to know a lot of our most challenging customers—particularly teens—better, and on a playing field where they feel more comfortable. Thanks to the frequent shopper card on my keychain, my supermarket will print out coupons for dog food instead of cat food on my receipts (although I honestly doubt that my dog would mind cat food as long as the bowl was filled). When I purchase a book or CD from Amazon.com, I get suggestions as to what other buyers who made similar purchases also bought. If automatic marketing devices enable companies to know their customers better, we should be able to surpass that with similar technology *plus* our "magic librarian ninja super skills."

Now that sites like MySpace and Facebook have given librarians an activity stream of what your teen customers have been up to, make certain to capitalize on that information to enhance how your library interacts with them. Whether it is simply wishing one of your teens a happy birthday after seeing an alert for it on your profile or adding CDs to your collection by artists whose songs that are frequently added to your teen friends' profiles, there are a variety of ways to capitalize on the information you get from social networking sites. While some are quick to call this the era of TMI, or Too Much Information, we, as librarians, should know that having an abundance of information is never a problem as long as you can rely on your navigation skills to get to what is of value.

When I began as a teen librarian, I was surprised to find that my library had blocked access to MySpace on the Internet accounts of minors. Sure, I was familiar with the somewhat overblown response in the media and government to the threat to young people from online predators, and I understood that news stories, pending legislation, and public opinion can exert a powerful influence on library policy. Still, it seemed unfair that an online phenomenon that had been so widely embraced by teens would be essentially prohibited to them. Luckily, when I spoke with my library director about this, he not only agreed and had the blocks removed but gave the go-ahead for the library teenspace to build a presence on My-Space. Since we broke virtual dirt in spring of 2006, we've made over 300 friends and had over 9,000 views of our profile. Whether it's MySpace, Facebook, or both, don't miss out on the opportunity to reach your teen customers and to aid in their development through the use of social networking sites. In the words of Anäis Nin, "Each friend represents a world in us, a world possibly not born until they arrive, and it is only by this meeting that a new world is born" (1967, 193).

REFERENCES

Chan, Jackie. *Jackie Chan's Who Am I?* DVD. Directed by Jackie Chan. Culver City, CA: Sony Pictures, 1998.

Hall, G. "Teens and Technology: Preparing for the Future." *New Directions for Youth Development* 111 (2006): 41–52.

Harris, S. "Run to the Hills." From *The Number of the Beast,* performed by Iron Maiden. London: EMI Harvest, 1982.

Lenhart, A. "The Democratization of Online Social Networks." Washington, DC: Pew Internet & American Life Project, 2009, http://www.pewinternet.org/Presentations/2009/41—The-Democratization-of-Online-Social-Networks.aspx/ (accessed February 22, 2010).

McElhaney, K., J. Antonishak, and J. Allen. "'They Like Me, They Like Me Not': Popularity and Adolescents' Perceptions of Acceptance Predicting Social Functioning Over Time." *Child Development* 79, no. 3 (2008): 720–31.

National Institute of Mental Health. "Teenage Brain: A Work in Progress." Washington, DC: National Institute of Mental Health, 2001, http://www.nimh.nih.gov/publicat/teenbrain.cfm/ (accessed February 22, 2010).

Nin, Anäis. *The Diary of Anais Nin,* vol. 2 (1934–1939). Orlando, FL: Harcourt Brace, 1967.

Wartella, E., A. Caplovitz, and J. Lee. "From Baby Einstein to Leapfrog, from Doom to the Sims, from Instant Messaging to Internet Chat Rooms: Public Interest in the Role of Interactive Media in Children's Lives." *Social Policy Report* 18, no. 4 (2004): 1–19.

WEBSITES

Facebook, http://www.facebook.com/
Farkle, http://www.facebook.com/apps/application.php?id=64571521476/
MySpace, http://www.myspace.com/
Partnership for 21st Century Skills, www.21stcenturyskills.org/

4

◇ ◇ ◇

THE ROLE OF MEDIA LITERACY EDUCATION WITHIN SOCIAL NETWORKING AND THE LIBRARY

Belinha S. De Abreu

I look at the technology that kids bring to school and try to harness that. You can either ban iPods (and cell phones, Blackberries or MP3s) or fill them with content. What do they have in their bookbags that we're not letting them use?

Karl Schaefer, North Carolina's Durham
Academy (Ramaswami 2008)

"DA lingo ppl use 2 txt n msg is not n fact bad 4 da lngwij skiLz of 2dayz teens" (Wilson 2008). Can you decipher what this text-based sentence is saying? Most adults are unable to do so at the first try, but many of today's teens use this form of text language frequently through the various social networking tools they are using. This sentence appeared in a newspaper article in *The Australian*, asking its readers to translate it into our everyday spoken English. The emphasis of the article was that language has changed tremendously and that text language is used primarily by this teen generation. It further led the readers into a discussion on a recent study of the beneficial uses of text language. The study findings showed that far from being detrimental, text language and emoticons have changed the thinking processes of our youth in positive ways (Wilson 2008).

Text language is just one of the positive outputs of social networking. There are many other outputs that can be considered beneficial. Whether

in a school or library, social networking provides opportunities for engagement in critical thinking and aligns well with media literacy education.
This chapter explores those ideas and shows how we can bring these tools
used primarily in the home into the school and the library.

MEDIA LITERACY AND SOCIAL NETWORKING

Whether it is cell phones with their new applications or social networking
sites such as *MySpace* or *Facebook*, today's youth are using these tools to create another communication and learning platform that is not used in many
schools or libraries across the United States (Boyd 2008). In December 2008,
roughly 125 million users visited MySpace, which indicates the immensity
of this site (Elsworth 2009). During that same month Facebook, MySpace's
main competition, had more than 220 million visitors (Elsworth 2009).
Many of these visitors are middle and high school teenagers, although more
and more kids as young as fourth- and fifth-graders are using these tools.
Clearly, the world of social networking has taken off to the point where it
is part of today's common everyday language and experiences. It is, in fact
teens', primary medium of choice (Roberts, Foehr, and Rideout 2005).

Look around any teenager's bedroom and you will see what gives him
or her a frame of reference for the world—the media. From the Internet,
television, radio, the iPod, and DVDs to video games, a child's life is dominated by the messages communicated via these platforms. Media texts are
ubiquitous for this generation of learners. They have a significant impact
on their lives, and social networking is a huge part of that impact (Lenhart
et al. 2007; Roberts, Foehr, and Rideout 2005).

It is, in fact, the influx of new media which suggests that media literacy
education is a vital part of a student's learning cycle. Silverblatt (2001)
provides one of the most comprehensive definitions of media literacy.
It extends beyond the elements of critical thinking but also includes an
awareness of media content through the following:

> The development of strategies with which to discuss and analyze
> media messages; an awareness of media content as "text" that provides
> insight into our contemporary culture and ourselves; the cultivation
> of an enhanced enjoyment, understanding, and appreciation of media
> content; and in the case of media communicator, the ability to produce
> effective and responsible media messages. (Silverblatt 2001, 120)

While this definition may seem complex, there are four basic tenets that
can be taken from it. Media literacy is the ability to (1) access, (2) analyze,

(3) evaluate, and (4) communicate information in a variety of forms and formats. These terms are recognized as being a part of Bloom's Taxonomy, which promotes the concept of critical thinking at its highest level (Anderson and Sosniak 1994).

In part due to social networking, today's teens are learning technology at a far more rapid pace than most adults. This fact has always been true, but it is significantly apparent now. Perhaps the main difference is that the key to many of these teens' modes of learning involves the process of socialization presented by the various technological platforms. Teens' relationships and their forms of sharing information depend on the continuous flow of information, which begins when they take what they learn and then bring it to the attention of their friends. Their friends, in turn, pass it on and the cycle continues. Yet there are too few conversations happening that question the content or context of this form of communication.

Social networking sites have in fact helped to create an online culture where teens create content and all participate in its creation. Henry Jenkins of MIT would say that this is what makes social networking such an important facet of teenage life. This "participatory culture," as he defines it, is one with "relatively low barriers to artistic expression and civic engagement, strong support of creating and sharing one's creations, and some type of informal mentorship whereby what is known by the most experienced is passed along to novices" (Jenkins 2006).

Teens are learning every day and their learning is active, but it does deviate from the structure of many schools' curriculums across the United States. Because of this division and the slow pace at which most schools are recognizing these tools for educational purposes, libraries have an opportunity for creating centers of learning that are based on social networking technologies. The library as a provider of information resources can legitimize the use of these tools by creating opportunities in which critical thinking skills can be employed.

The question becomes how do librarians—whether in the public or school library—and educators teach and learn through social networking? In answering this question, it is important to understand the behaviors of teens and their social networks.

- 93% of U.S. teens aged 12 to 17 go online.
- 73% of U.S. teens aged 12 to 17 who do go online use social networks such as MySpace and Facebook.
- 75% of U.S. teens aged 12 to 17 have a cell phone (Lenhart et al. 2010).

These statistics demonstrate how important this form of socializing has become to teens and its relevancy to their daily lives. The online environment has become a place where teens can create content through blogging, video uploads, gaming, and much more (Goodstein 2007). It has become a place for them to identify themselves and even create a new persona. A PBS *Frontline* documentary titled "Growing Up Online" covered this topic in depth and showed how easy it was for teens to craft their lives around the online world without their parents seeing it happen. The documentary presented a scary viewpoint, and it handled the topic with just enough fear to capture its audience. However, surrounding those cautionary stories were also more positive stories that showed how much teens were able to work through these social programs, grow, and learn because the platforms were able to keep their attention for hours when the classroom was not doing so (Dretzin 2008).

Students' online creations and text language have added to the general world discussion and taken on a life of their own. In doing so, social networking has left behind the skeptics who had previously believed that these online programs served no purpose except child's play. There is research indicating that teens' literacy lives outside of school are quite different from their literacy lives inside of school (Boyd 2008). In fact, it is still difficult for some parents and educators to recognize that new media environments fall under the umbrella of literacy. Besides enabling teens to work on their reading and writing skills, many of these technological platforms also provide for creating, collaborating, and much more.

Researchers studying new literacies have been able to show that, with each new technological advance, more knowledge has been gained than lost. The issue that arises is that in most schools and even libraries, the focus on the actual technology becomes much more important than the work that comes through the use of the technology. Yet data collected demonstrate that teens can be quite skilled as online readers. Through their own interests, students are able to search online and move from site to site in a well-organized manner (Coiro 2009). In retrospect, what stands out is that teens' abilities to critically evaluate and analyze online material is limited because there are few conversations that ask them to interpret or evaluate any given message.

Media literacy teaches teens to look at these communication environments with fresh eyes. By looking at what learning outcomes have resulted from social network use—such as the text-based language made up of symbols and letters or emoticons, which help teens to communicate a sentiment or feeling without the need for any words at all—educational legitimacy has been established (Goodstein 2007).

Social networking sites have given teens a platform for identification, creation, communication, and collaboration, which are very important parts of this generation's everyday interactions (Boyd 2008). At a recent American Association of School Libraries (AASL) conference, Boyd, a leading researcher in the area of social networking, stated that the Internet and social networking sites are highlighting issues that adults have ignored for centuries: the social hierarchy of high school and other teen issues. She also suggested that the Internet makes it difficult to ignore racial divides and bullying when the actions of teens escalate due to their online activities. In fact, she recommended that teachers and those who work with youth get online with their students. Thus, librarians and educators should have social networking profiles that they use in an educational capacity—allowing their students to see them and to connect with them online.

SOCIAL NETWORKING IN
THE POPULAR MEDIA

The popular media have taken notice of the overwhelming popularity of social networking and are now using it to push forward their messages. Popular mainstream music creators as well as major advertisers have begun to incorporate text language and to use social networking sites as a means of communicating with youth (Holson 2008). Many popular songs refer to social networking sites within the context of the lyrics. One artist who has done this is Mariah Carey (2008). In the song entitled, "Touch My Body," Carey sings about dating and having her relationships displayed on a popular social medium, YouTube. It is amazing to think that just a few short years ago many of us would not even know of this network, yet today almost every child and teen—as well as most adults—has viewed, previewed, or posted a video on YouTube (Goodstein 2007). Here again, media literacy education would help teens to analyze the messages presented and also to observe the integration of language through symbolism, or it might even be used to teach Internet safety—an important topic for today's youth.

As another example, Degree Girl deodorant launched its recent advertising campaign with teen superstar Ashley Tisdale, best known for her role in *High School Musical*, with the text, "For Your OMG Moments." The campaign included Tisdale "vlogging" with teens about her own OMG moments. Vlogging is a combination of video and blogging, which allows Tisdale to be present in person while also texting.

The Degree Girl deodorant campaign is not the only one to use teen speak and text language. McDonalds has created a campaign with the motto "R U Ready." Also, cell phone companies, which have provided the service that allows teens to text, have created advertising campaigns emphasizing this new text language. AT&T is on the forefront with its "IDK, My BFF Rose" campaign, which reaches from teens to the aged using subtitled conversation between mom, daughter, and grandmother on the overuse of texting via cell phone and the money it costs them (Holson 2008).

WHAT ABOUT LIBRARIES?

Do these content creators and social networks have a place in our libraries? Yes. In fact, here is where teens can have the freedom to participate in these online environments without interruption. One of the first libraries to recognize the importance of creating teen digital spaces was the Chicago Public Library. In conjunction with the John D. and Catherine T. MacArthur Foundation and the Pearson Foundation, they created a real-time public space for teens called YOUMedia. YOUMedia "is home to thousands of books, more than 100 laptop and desktop computers, and a variety of media creation tools and software, including a recording studio, which allows teens to express through music and spoken word" (Web Newswire 2009). A virtual space was also created to extend the connection with young adults through an online community. The success of this recent project cannot be determined yet, but this library has begun moving in the right direction by considering its audience of teens.

The idea for this digital space came from a comprehensive ethnographic study of 700 youth, headed by Professor Mizuko Ito at the University of California, Berkeley. It found that teens engage in media in three primary ways: "(1) they 'hang out' with friends in social spaces such as Facebook and MySpace; (2) they 'mess around' or tinker with digital media, making simple videos, playing online games, or posting pictures in Flickr; and (3) they 'geek out' in online groups that facilitate exploration of their core interests" (Ito 2008). Bringing all those elements into a space provided through the Chicago Public Library allows for librarians to create projects that will promote creativity and critical thinking.

While what is exemplified by the Chicago Public Library is without question a step in the right direction, many other libraries have encountered various barriers to incorporating social networking into their services for teens. Some of the more common issues have to do with Internet policies, individuals discounting social networking as a form of learning, others not finding such networking to be an effective communications tool, and still others just plain being unknowledgeable about the potential educational benefits of social networking.

Librarians and educators who discount the value of social networking tend to fall into two categories: those who are not using it and those who are not sure how to use it (Richardson 2004). Those who are not using it need training and the time to actually play in some of these sites. One of the biggest benefits and educational opportunities is the possibility for collaboration among librarians, teachers, and students. The ideas of putting students into groups on some of these platforms and working on a science experiment or developing a context for reading groups under a blog are very real possibilities that currently exist within some of these sites. Establishing opportunities for students to work cooperatively is one of the easiest ways of engaging students in these areas.

In some cases, those who see social networking as an ineffective communication tool are stumped by the text language that has developed along with the growth of these sites. Researchers are beginning to look at the potential of learning processes, whether informal or formal, taking place through online chat or instant messaging:

> Online chat and instant messaging require very specific skills in language and interpersonal communication. Young people have to learn to "read" subtle nuances, often on the basis of minimal cues. They have to learn the rules and etiquette of online communication and to shift quickly between genres or language registers. (Buckingham 2007, 100)

Emoticons and the shorthand version of the English language, inspired by acronyms, say a lot about the pace at which communication and social networking have reached the public. At the same time, these new literacies determine the process of thinking, which permits teens to create, decode, and produce a unique language that they share throughout their social networks of choice. Incorporating these digital forms of reading and writing into libraries and classrooms may seem like a bad idea to some, but it poses the risk of creating a major divide if ignored. Step away from schools and libraries, and this form of language is already in use by business executives and employees who use it daily in the form of letters, acronyms, and emoticons. As the world changes in moving further into the 21st century, so must we change in the way we teach reading, writing, visual, and media literacy within the context of the classroom and the library.

That is, the line between classic written language and text language is beginning to blur. Teachers from various curricular areas have begun to see an influx of text language in written homework turned in by students, and they tend to look upon this with grave concern. Yet, the potential for learning exists, and tapping into that area opens up new teaching and learning possibilities. For example, Canadian linguists have found that these new forms of speech allow youth to show what they can do with language (Wilson 2008).

CONCLUSION

In a Web 2.0 world, the main goal is for students, educators, and librarians to connect, access, analyze, evaluate, and create on digital platforms while forming communities of learning with shared interests. This requires, by technological design, a partnership in which the flow of information can exist and that sounds very much like media literacy in its conventional form. There is an obvious correlation here, as media literacy is about thinking and evaluating the media in all forms. Web 2.0 is therefore just another structure by which media literacy learning becomes applicable. In fact, media literacy promotes critical thinking beyond the traditional literacies of reading and writing, since it includes both visual and computer literacies.

Potter (2005) suggests that these literacies are the key components of the greater thought on what media literacy is:

> Media literacy is a set of perspectives that we actively use to expose ourselves to the media to interpret the meaning of the messages we encounter. We build our perspectives from knowledge structures. To build our structures, we need tools and raw material. These tools are our skills. The raw materials are information from the media and from the real world. Active use means that we are aware of the messages and consciously interacting with them. (22)

Last, in a recent article, Adam Newman from *Outsell*, a market research firm serving publishers and information providers, stated,

> There are two ways to think: "How do you protect the kids from the technology?" OR, "How do you unlock the creativity of the kids by engaging them with technology?" If you assume that students will

get their hands into the cookie jar, you're thinking about it the wrong way. (Ramaswami 2008)

Newman's words clearly make the point that librarians, teachers, and parents need to seek out the doorways into these new technologies. These computer programs, tools, and social networking sites are rooted deeply within teens' daily lives and will not soon go away. Providing media literacy education through the use of these social networking tools opens a doorway into their worlds, and the library can become a wide-open portal for educational opportunities.

REFERENCES

Anderson, Lorin, and Lauren Sosniak. "Bloom's Taxonomy: A Forty-Year Retrospective." *Ninety-Third Yearbook of the National Society for the Study of Education,* Pt. 2. Chicago: University of Chicago Press, 1994.

Boyd, Danah. "Why Youth (Heart) Social Network Sites: The Role of Networked Publics in Teenage Social Life." In *Youth, Identity, and Digital Media.* The John D. and Catherine T. MacArthur Foundation Series on Digital Media and Learning, edited by David Buckingham, 119–42. Cambridge, MA: MIT Press, 2008.

Buckingham, David. *Beyond Technology: Children's Learning in the Age of Digital Culture.* Cambridge, MA: Polity Press, 2007.

Carey, Mariah. "Touch My Body." *E = MC2,* CD. New York: Island Records, 2008.

Coiro, Julie. "Rethinking Online Reading Assessment." *Educational Leadership* 66, no. 6 (March 2009): 59–63.

Dretzin, Rachel, writer, director, and producer. "Growing Up Online." *Frontline.* New York: PBS, 2008.

Elsworth, Catherine. "Facebook Draws Twice as Many Visitors as MySpace." January 23, 2009, http://www.telegraph.co.uk/technology/facebook/4327369/Facebook-draws-twice-as-many-visitors-as-MySpace.html/ (accessed February 24, 2010).

Goodstein, Anastasia. *Totally Wired: What Teens and Tweens Are Really doing Online.* New York: St. Martin's Griffin, 2007.

Holson, Laura M. "Text Generation Gap: U R 2 Old (JK)." *The New York Times,* March 9, 2008, http://www.nytimes.com/2008/03/09/business/09cell.html/ (accessed February 23, 2010).

Ito, Mizuko. "Living and Learning with New Media: Summary of Findings from the Digital Youth Project." Chicago: The John D. and Catherine T. MacArthur Foundation. November 2008, http://www.macfound.org/atf/cf/%7BB0386CE3–8B29–4162–8098-E466FB856794%7D/DML_ETHNOG_WHITEPAPER.PDF/ (accessed February 24, 2010).

Jenkins, Henry. "Confronting the Challenges of Participatory Culture: Media Education for the 21st Century." October 2006, http://www.henryjenkins.org/2006/10/confronting_the_challenges_of.html/ (accessed February 24, 2010).

Lenhart, Amanda, Mary Madden, Aaron Smith, and Alexandra Macgill. "Teens and Social Media." Washington, DC: Pew Internet & American Life Project, December 19, 2007, http://www.pewinternet.org/Reports/2007/Teens-and-Social-Media.aspx/ (accessed February 24, 2010).

Lenhart, Amanda, Kristen Purcell, Aaron Smith, and Kathryn Zickuhr. "Social Media and Young Adults." Washington, DC: Pew Internet & American Life Project, February 3, 2010, http://pewinternet.org/Reports/2010/Social-Media-and-Young-Adults.aspx/ (accessed July 21, 2010).

Potter, W. James. *Media Literacy,* 3rd ed. Thousand Oaks, CA: Sage Publications, 2005.

Ramaswami, Rama. "Fill 'Er Up," *T.H.E. Journal.* May 1, 2008, http://www.the journal.com/articles/22571/ (accessed February 24, 2010).

Richardson, Will. "Blogging and RSS—The 'What's It?' and 'How To' of Powerful New Web Tools for Educators." *MultiMedia & Internet@Schools* 11, no 1 (January/February 2004), http://www.infotoday.com/MMSchools/jan04/richardson.shtml/ (accessed February 24, 2010).

Roberts, Donald, Ulla Foehr, and Victoria Rideout. "Generation M: Media in the Lives of 8–18 Year-Olds." *A Kaiser Family Foundation Study.* March 2005, http://www.kff.org/entmedia/upload/Generation-M-Media-in-the-Lives-of-8–18-Year-olds-Report.pdf/ (accessed February 24, 2010).

Silverblatt, Art. *Media Literacy: Keys to Interpreting Media Messages.* Westport, CT: Praeger, 2001.

Web Newswire. "Mayor Daley and Chicago Public Library Offers Teens Digital Media Space." October 20, 2009, http://www.webnewswire.com/node/473609 (accessed February 24, 2010).

Wilson, Lauren. "Txt Msg Lingo Defended." *The Australian News,* May 15, 2008, http://www.theaustralian.news.com.au.story.0.25197.23700796–2702.00.html/ (accessed February 24, 2010).

WEBSITE

YOUMedia, www.youmediachicago.org/

5

◇ ◇ ◇

IF YOU BUILD IT, WILL THEY COME? A COMPARISON OF SOCIAL NETWORKING UTILITIES

Stephanie D. Reynolds

Judging by the articles in recent professional journals on my desk, social networking may be taking over libraries and education. Some examples include Kate Messner's "Pleased to Tweet You: Making a Case for Twitter in the Classroom" (2009) and Karen Coombs's "Drupal Done Right: Libraries Using This Open Source Content Management System Pioneer New Tools and Services" (2009). In her "In Practice" column for *American Libraries*, Meredith Farkas presents "Governing Social Media: Protect Your Library's Brand Online" (2009). And more on topic, in *VOYA*'s "Electronic Eye" column, Kathleen Muelen offers "Web 2.0, Social Networking, and the YouTube Generation" (2009).

It would seem that social networking is the way to bring teens into the library—and not just virtually. Articles and reviews aside, any regular user of social networking can easily see that the lines between different types and brands of social networking tools have begun to blur. Once stand-alone products, Twitter feeds and blogs are now incorporated into many other social networking products. If they are not incorporated into the application itself, they are easily streamed in, thus making it less necessary to abandon existing avenues of social networking when new tools are introduced.

Many libraries are making use of multiple social networking avenues for engaging patrons of all ages, such as using Twitter to lead patrons to their Facebook pages. Even the American Library Association (ALA) has gotten into the social networking business. In addition to the official ALA website, the Young Adult Library Services Association (YALSA) maintains Facebook and MySpace pages, a blog, and a Twitter presence, as well as a Student Interest Group Ning.

WHY ENGAGE: TO BUILD OR NOT TO BUILD

Many public libraries are already using online social networking sites to engage teens in literary discussions and, with any luck, to bring them running in to check out the latest hot titles. But which types of tools are they using? And are sites such as Facebook, MySpace, and LiveJournal the best options for libraries, or is setting up a blog or Ning a better choice? Keep reading to learn which tools are the most popular with libraries interested in engaging teens, which receive the most traffic from teens, and why such engagement is important. This chapter also evaluates the functionality of each type of social networking tool, including ease of customization and which long-standing providers offer the best options for libraries, including security settings and forced moderation.

VIRTUAL FOUNDATIONS: A VIEW OF THE LANDSCAPE

One of the major differences between the various social networking platforms is the inclusion of a friends network—a community of users who read and comment on each other's online content. While Facebook and MySpace, as well as Nings, support interaction among the community members, blogs typically do not. While blogs typically are signed, most allow for nonidentifying user names. Some social networking utilities include both community-based and individual forums. Additional information about these tools and about a number of other popular social networking platforms follows.

Facebook and MySpace

Starting with the largest of the social networking communities, Facebook and MySpace bring people together based on conditions such as common geography (city or employer), common interests (favorite author or band), and common history (alma mater or former employer).

As indicated in the Introduction, Facebook has surpassed MySpace as the most popular social networking site, with 77 million unique U.S. visitors in June 2009 (Rao 2009). If a quick perusal of MySpace is any indication, we don't need statistics to tell us why its popularity is declining. While the flashy pages may attract teens, pages that are difficult to view and navigate deter repeat visitors. MySpace does offer more control of content, but too many of those responsible for designing and maintaining the pages do not want that level of control or are not willing to invest enough time to maintain MySpace pages.

Nings

As mentioned, the social networking product lines have begun to blur, and some platforms are not the stand-alone products that they once were. Nings, which are social networks based on a common theme, have blogging options available, and Twitter feeds can be streamed in as well. Though not a library site, one Ning popular with teens and the adults who serve them is that of Hank and John Green—Nerdfighters, where they blog, video blog (vlog) with streaming live videos, stream their respective Twitter feeds, make use of the discussion board, and link out to their wiki.

The advantages of using Nings are many. Nings are quite easy to set up and maintain. They also offer a sense of community that is perhaps safer than Facebook and MySpace, and, as mentioned, allow for the integration of other social networking products, including Facebook. On the other hand, integration can create management problems for library staff.

Nings offer limited privacy settings but tight membership controls. Based on an informal review of a number of library Nings designed to engage teens, it is evident that few require users to sign in to view posts. However, one must usually sign in to post comments. Ning sites allow you to use of your own domain name for a monthly fee, and they can support polls, Word Press, Hulu, news sharing, RSS feeds, and chat functions.

Nings also enable the creation of subgroups, which is great for libraries that want to target specific groups of teens without setting up separate groups altogether (as would be necessary with Facebook and MySpace). So if a library happens to have some teens who love mysteries and some who love science fiction, for example, the Ning can be set up with two distinct discussion groups.

Drupal

Drupal websites are content-managed sites that function in much the same way as Nings but allow for greater manipulation of content. Drupal allows for both discussion forums and blogs, and Twitter feeds can be streamed in. It is difficult to tell by just looking at a library's site if it is built on the Drupal platform because such sites look like regular websites. Those familiar with ALA Connect will note that it uses the Drupal platform.

While Drupal sites can be effective communication forums, response time to Drupal posts can be slow. Teens might become frustrated if they think there is no activity, only to log in one day and discover an abundance of "new" posts that they missed. Such delays may be the result of institutional server issues and not problems due to Drupal functionality.

In addition, the design and maintenance of a Drupal-based site requires knowledge of HTML and other elements of website design. This likely makes the Drupal platform less desirable for smaller libraries that lack a technology person or someone with the skills (not to mention the time) necessary to manage the site. For a list of libraries using Drupal, see the websites at the end of this chapter.

Blogs

Blogs, which are essentially public journals, are for sharing thoughts and ideas in a virtual venue that solicits feedback. While fairly popular, blogs do not have the overall functionality offered by Nings and Drupal sites, but again, they are easily integrated into library websites. Blogs are easy to maintain, allow for easy moderation of posts and can be set to require registration to post. Blogger and WordPress are two of the most popular free blogging platforms. The official YALSA blog is powered by WordPress. Typepad is another popular blog platform that requires a minimum monthly fee, which may not be affordable for small public libraries.

LiveJournal

LiveJournal is essentially a blog with a friends' network and thus much like a Ning. It is popular with many young adult authors, but most of them are using it in conjunction with other applications. LiveJournal has some nice features, such as an instant messenger and extensive user settings, but all of the options can be overwhelming.

People and organizations can create a network of friends just as with Facebook, MySpace, and Nings, but otherwise LiveJournal functions just as a blog does. Blog posts can be updated to Facebook automatically. In some respects, LiveJournal has the most promise for libraries to engage teens. However, library staff might have concerns regarding recent "enhancements." When you click the "friend" link on a LiveJournal page, for example, you are taken to friends' pages to read their blog posts. It can be a never-ending cycle, which means that not just your friends but anyone using LiveJournal can access your content.

Twitter

Twitter is the ultimate in electronic instant social gratification and perhaps has the most potential for engaging teens. It has taken a while to catch on, but desktop and iPhone applications for Twitter now abound. Not only has Twitter become a regular part of our vernacular, but so have "tweets" and "tweeps," as well as "hashtags" (#hashtag). Hashtags are metadata for tweets, and they allow for trend following. Trend following allows users to see what hot topics people are twittering about. The popularity of trend following is big part of the appeal of Twitter. Anyone can establish a hashtag, whether it be to follow tweets about their favorite Hollywood star, a favorite author, genre, or book title (just to name a few). Libraries can establish a hashtag for a particular discussion topic and use TweetChat to run an ongoing or time-limited discussion about a book, an author, or a literary genre.

Twitter allows for the immediate exchange of ideas, but an incessant flow of Twitter posts can be taxing. Its limit of 140 characters per post helps to minimize overload (though some users get around that limit with multiple tweets). Unlike e-mail, Twitter posts do not accumulate and do not require maintenance or deletion.

But do teens use Twitter? The online social media guide *Mashable* reported in August 2009 that teens do not tweet (Cashmore 2009). The chat room environment, accessible using sites such as TweetChat, may soon attract more teens to Twitter, especially since the chat format offers more anonymity than the regular Twitter open environment. Regardless, some libraries do use Twitter to interact with teens. Most of the libraries using Twitter to engage teens primarily link them back to a website, Ning, or blog. For example, see the Lancaster Public Library (in Pennsylvania) Twitter page and the Farmington Public Library (in New Mexico) Twitter page.

Privacy Concerns

As with book selection, the responsibility for educating teens about online privacy issues ultimately falls to parents or other guardians. However, libraries should still keep in mind the privacy settings of the social networking platforms being considered for use with teens. For example, can users be anonymous or have a user name other than their real name? Can posts be moderated? Can networks be controlled, and do they require user verification? None of the platforms currently available can say yes to all of these questions.

Facebook and MySpace

Facebook and MySpace come with a myriad of privacy concerns, and their never-ending attempts to improve upon privacy settings make it difficult to assess the overall threat to privacy and to identity protection. Both sites require users to supply their real names to register. Many teens (as well as many adults) unwittingly include their full date of birth on their personal profiles, making them more vulnerable to identity theft. Facebook implemented updated privacy settings in December 2009 that allow for greater control of personal information, but they are only effective if the user is aware that owing to those recent changes, some data that were not visible before are now publicly visible. On December 18, 2009, the American Library Association filed a joint complaint with the Federal Trade Commission stating that the changes to Facebook's privacy settings violated consumer protection laws (*District Dispatch* 2009). By the time you read this book, the settings likely will have changed again—for better or worse. MySpace and Google Buzz (Google's plunge into the social network realm) have recently been experiencing similar privacy issues.

Nings

Ning sites, which are growing in popularity, allow administrators to require identity verification before a user is accepted to a group. Student networks are ad-free. Others can obtain an ad-free site for a fee. There are many different privacy settings, and each Ning owner must take the time to explore and implement the appropriate settings. Site membership is required in order to post comments on sites, but will teens feel comfortable making comments if they know that anyone can see what they have written? On the other hand, Nings do allow for user names, so they offer more anonymity than Facebook and MySpace.

Library organizations using Nings need to be willing to spend the time that verification of users requires, especially if they are going to use the site with minors. This means that if a library has a Ning for general patron use, the teens should have a separate site. While teens need to be educated to understand the potential threats of using any social networking platform, platforms such as Nings that require membership can give anyone a false sense of security. The "friending" aspect of many social networking sites can also be problematic. Young people may feel obligated to accept a friend request despite feeling uncomfortable about doing so. Libraries can offer classes to teens (and adults) educating them on social networking safety and etiquette.

Drupal

Drupal allows for a range of privacy settings similar to that of Nings, but the settings are not as simple to understand, making privacy issues a drawback to Drupal for use with teens. Member groups can be tightly controlled, and "friending" can be enabled. Individual entries can be set for public viewing or can be kept private to the user.

Blogs

As with any of the social networking applications, the privacy settings for blogs vary. Comment moderation is a standard feature of most blogging platforms, but each has unique aspects. For example, WordPress has a setting that makes a blog completely private. A WordPress blog can be excluded from search engine results as well as allow for invitation-only use. WordPress users can adopt anonymous user names, and blog age ratings are available using the same basic scale as the Motion Picture Association of America. Automatic content restrictions also are possible.

Blogger, which is a Google product, is somewhat more limited than WordPress. There is an adult-content selector, but no other age ratings are available. Blogger allows for CAPTCHA (word verification) to reduce spam, whereas WordPress does not. (More information on word verification protocols is given at the CAPTCHA website.) Both sites support OpenID, which allows users with accounts that support OpenID (e.g., Facebook, MySpace, Google, WordPress, Yahoo!, and LiveJournal) to use that information to automatically log into other OpenID-supported applications. The use of OpenID might make a library's blog more accessible for teens, but it opens the door for unintended users.

Blogging remains quite popular, but tracking participation while protecting participants continues to be a challenge.

LiveJournal

With LiveJournal, Blog entries can be exported to Facebook, posts can be moderated, CAPTCHA is available, and anonymous comments are permissible. However, there are several substantial privacy concerns.

One of those concerns is LiveJournal's "My Guest" feature, which allows page owners to see who has visited their pages. This feature is a bit too "big brother" for comfort, especially when there are minors involved. LiveJournal also offers IP tracking, which could be beneficial for assessment purposes, but it could present liability issues for libraries.

Another concern is the feature that permits notification of "unfriending." Most people are sensitive to rejection, and the virtual world does not offer immunity from such feelings. While any of us might notice that we have been "unfriended" when our friend count changes, receiving notification could be worse and could cause unnecessary friction, especially in a closed community.

Twitter

Instead of using a friend system, Twitter uses a follower system that allows members to receive live feeds of a person's tweets. Twitter does have a problem with follower requests from adult-content providers, but privacy settings permit users to require the approval of potential followers. Twitter also asks users for a real name for registration, but it will accept nicknames and first names only. TweetChat does not circumvent any of the privacy settings established with Twitter, and the TweetChat connection can be managed from within the Twitter account. For teens who want to avoid revealing too much personal information online and who are selective in whom they allow as followers, Twitter appears to be a relatively safe bet.

CONCLUSION: IT ALL COMES DOWN TO ENGAGING TEEN LIBRARY USERS

We must consider whether teens will be turned off by library tools that require too much effort for them to join in. Most of the libraries that have embraced social networking have realized that to reach patrons, young and old alike, the use of multiple platforms is necessary to increase the likelihood that users will interact with the library in online environments that they already use. Platform integration has made that easier. Blog users can now post entries to Facebook, and Twitter feeds can be incorporated into almost any social networking application. (Nings will supposedly support that function soon.) Polls are one feature now available for most social networking applications, and many teens seem to like creating and taking online polls. Blogs, Nings, and Facebook allow for teens to vote on books, take part in mock book award elections, and the like. Even on teen library sites and pages where teens are not responding to posts and requests for feedback, many are voting in these kinds of polls.

New features such as these are likely to increase teens' interest in social networking, and they provide easy programming options for libraries looking to engage teens online. Ultimately, libraries must have a presence where the teens are if they want to engage them. Privacy matters very little if there is no one there to protect, and social networking provides an opportunity to teach the responsible use of technology. If multiple platform integration will allow easier access to sites where teens do not have an account, they are more likely to participate in library programs and services. OpenID may also may help to overcome this potential hurdle.

Other possibilities for libraries to consider are social networking sites just for readers, such as GoodReads, Shelfari, and LibraryThing (see chapter 8 for a deeper discussion of these sites). It is hard to know the future of social networking and how it will figure into the lives of teens and the libraries that serve them, but teens will not come if libraries do not build tools that engage them and that, at the very least, respect their need for privacy. That is, after all, what being an adolescent is all about.

REFERENCES

Cashmore, Pete. "Stats Confirm It: Teens Don't Tweet." (August 5, 2009), http://mashable.com/2009/08/05/teens-dont-tweet/ (accessed December 5, 2009).

Coombs, Karen. "Drupal Done Right: Libraries Using This Open Source Content Management System Pioneer New Tools and Services." *Library Journal* 19 (November 15, 2009), http://www.libraryjournal.com/article/CA6705363.html/ (accessed November 17, 2009).

District Dispatch. "ALA Joins Electronic Privacy Information Center in Complaint against Facebook Privacy Changes," http://www.wo.ala.org/districtdispatch/?p=4171/ (accessed December 18, 2009).

Farkas, Meredith. "Governing Social Media: Protect your Library's Brand Online." *American Libraries* 40 (December 2009): 35.

Messner, Kate. "Pleased to Tweet You: Making a Case for Twitter in the Classroom." *School Library Journal* 55 (December 1, 2009): 44.

Muelen, Kathleen. "Web 2.0, Social Networking, and the YouTube Generation." *Voice of Youth Advocates,* 2009, http://pdfs.voya.com/VO/YA2/VOYA 200912electronic-eye.pdf/ (accessed November 29, 2009).

Rao, L. "The Gap Grows Wider: MySpace Eats Facebook's Dust in the U.S." *Techcrunch* (July 13, 2009), http://www.techcrunch.com/2009/07/13/the-gap-grows-wider-myspace-eats-facebooks-dust-in-the-us/ (accessed February 23, 2010).

WEBSITES

ALA Connect, http://connect.ala.org/
Blogger, http://www.blogger.com/
CAPTCHA, http://www.captcha.net/
Drupal, http://www.drupal.com/
Facebook, http://www.facebook.com/
Farmington Public Library Twitter page, http://twitter.com/FPLTeenZone/
GoodReads, http://www.goodreads.com/
Google Buzz, http://www.google.com/buzz/
Lancaster Public Library Twitter page, http://twitter.com/teenlibraryhub/
Libraries using Drupal, http://groups.drupal.org/libraries/libraries/
LibraryThing, http://www.librarything.com/
LiveJournal, http://www.livejournal.com/
MySpace, http://www.myspace.com/
Nerdfighters, http://nerdfighters.ning.com/
Nings, http://www.ning.com/
OpenID, http://openid.net/
Shelfari, http://www.shelfari.com/
TweetChat, http://tweetchat.com/
Twitter, http://www.twitter.com/
Typepad, http://www.typepad.com/
WordPress, http://www.wordpress.com/
Young Adult Library Services Association (YALSA) blog, http://yalsa.ala.org/blog/
Young Adult Library Services Association (YALSA) Facebook page, http://www.facebook.com/yalsa/
Young Adult Library Services Association (YALSA) MySpace page, http://www.myspace.com/yalsa/
Young Adult Library Services Association (YALSA) Twitter page, http://twitter.com/yalsa/
Young Adult Library Services Association (YALSA) Student Interest Group Ning, http://yalsasig.ning.com/

6

◈ ◈ ◈

TEENS, SOCIAL NETWORKING, AND SAFETY AND PRIVACY ISSUES

Denise E. Agosto and June Abbas

Throughout this book we show how social networks can be useful tools for connecting with teens. This is not to imply unconditional approval of these tools. As with most things, there are benefits and drawbacks to using social networks, as well as potential risks. Most importantly, librarians need to keep in mind that privacy and security are important issues to consider in designing and delivering online library services for young adults. Teens (and adults) might think of social networks as private spaces, but they are not truly private. Frequent articles in the popular press indicate that many adults worry about issues of information privacy and information security when it comes to online interactions and to posting information online, particularly in social networking environments. For example, in May 2010, the *New York Times* reported that an error in Facebook's information privacy controls made content that users thought was private viewable to all of their Facebook friends:

> On Wednesday, users discovered a glitch that gave them access to supposedly private information in the accounts of their Facebook friends, like chat conversations. . . . Although Facebook quickly moved to close the security hole on Wednesday, the breach heightened a feeling among many users that it was becoming hard to trust the service to protect their personal information. (Wortham 2010)

The point is that content posted in social networks becomes the property of the system's owners. As such, users cede at least partial rights to protecting the privacy of their personal information to social network owners and administrators.

On the one hand, information privacy and security issues are as old as society itself. On the other hand, it could be said that teens today face more possible risks to privacy and security than teens did in past generations, since such a large percentage of modern social interaction takes place online. Online communication often leaves written and visual records of interactions that previously would not have existed. This means that in today's highly networked world, more personal information is available to more people than ever before, and questions of personal privacy and information security must be considered. We must ask questions such as "What does 'privacy' mean in a highly networked world?" "Who owns personal information that is voluntarily posted online?" "How risky it is to post personal information online?" "Who has access to the information that we put online, and for how long?" and "What becomes of our information after it is posted in online communities?" These are difficult questions to answer. They are further complicated in the case of social networks, which by definition require the sharing of personal information for participation, and they are complicated still further when the social network users are minors.

In dealing with young people and issues of information privacy and security, additional questions arise, such as "How much control over their own personal information should youth have?" "How much should adults be able to enforce privacy and security restrictions on youth?" and "At what point are we protecting youth from possible dangers, and at what point are we restricting their rights to share and exchange information?"

Many popular press outlets have suggested that unlike adults, teens are not concerned with online privacy and security. These authors typically claim that teens are willing to put much more private information online than are adults, and that they do so with little regard to possible privacy and security risks (e.g., Havenstein 2008).

Our work with teens indicates that these claims just aren't true. Teens might be willing to put a great deal of personal information online, but most do care about information privacy and information security, as explained later in this chapter.

However, merely being concerned with issues of information privacy and security does not mean that teens as a group are private, safe users of social networks and other information communication technologies. Just as nearly "the entire population of adult Americans exhibits a high level of online privacy illiteracy" (Hoofnagle et al. 2010), teens are often confused by social network privacy setting options and often unaware of the security risks of posting personal information online. This is not to say that adults and teens share exactly the same ideas of privacy. Moscardelli and Liston-Heyes (2004) have suggested that the differences in ideas of privacy are tied to teens' lesser knowledge about privacy issues in general. As a result, understanding privacy and how to maintain privacy online is a learning process, and this makes teaching teens about privacy issues and potential security risks an important role for public and school librarians.

This chapter first discusses the major issues related to teens, social networking, and privacy and security issues. It then suggests ways in which librarians can help teens to protect their privacy online and help them to become safer users of social networks and other information communication technologies.

THE PRIVACY AND SECURITY CONFLICT: PROTECTING PERSONAL INFORMATION VERSUS ENGAGING IN ONLINE SHARING

Using a social networking site requires, by definition, "providing some sort of personal information in order to connect and communicate with other people" (Marwick et al. 2010, 29). Online social networking is an extension of social communication in the offline world, in which the sharing of personal information is crucial for building and maintaining peer relationships. As librarians, we must be careful not to judge teens negatively for sharing personal information in social networks any more than we would judge them negatively for socializing with peers in the offline world. We must remember that engaging in online information sharing is a healthy, normal part of the modern socialization process. As Marwick et al. (2010) wrote:

> Discussions of children and teens disclosing personal information [online] often take for granted that this provision is irrational or foolhardy. However, within the context of "real life" peer relationships, sharing personal information is normal and usual. This does not change for youth online. (24)

Nonetheless, many parents, librarians, teachers, members of the popular press, and other adults are quick to condemn teens for engaging in online exchanges of personal information. An important role for youth librarians lies in helping adults to understand that exchanging online information is generally a normal, healthy practice and a part of growing up in modern society.

This is not to suggest that teens should reveal all of their personal information online—far from it. Rather, we need to teach teens to think about the benefits of revealing personal information online versus the possible privacy and security risks.

The most basic method for protecting one's privacy in social networks is to use the system's privacy settings to restrict who has access to the user's personal information. Unfortunately, few if any social networks provide clearly written, straightforward privacy policies. Teens and adults alike often struggle to understand them and to choose the settings that best meet their needs. Facebook in particular has changed its privacy settings repeatedly over the years since its inception, incurring widespread criticism from privacy advocates (Fletcher 2010). At one point in early 2010, Facebook's privacy policy had "50 different settings and 170 options and [ran] to 5,830 words, making it longer than the U.S. Constitution" (BBC News 2010). This statement bears repeating: *Facebook's privacy policy was actually longer than the entire U.S. Constitution.* (The policy was shortened in mid-2010 in response to public protests.) No two social networks have exactly the same policies, forcing users of multiple communities to read and interpret multiple complicated documents. No wonder users of all ages struggle to understand privacy and security settings and are often unaware of how the companies that own the networks are using their personal information.

Even when teens can manage to interpret these complicated policies, selecting the most restrictive privacy settings available is not enough to maximize online privacy and security. No matter how tightly teens control the personal information they post online, there still may be privacy and security risks if they share information with online friends. These risks can be caused by online friends reusing their information without their permission. As Lohr has explained, "You may not disclose personal information, but your online friends and colleagues may do it for you, referring to your school or employer, gender, location, and interests" (Lohr 2010, A1). A teen might post a personal story or photo and be unaware that an online friend will share it more widely via any number of means: within the same social network enabling a different group of friends to gain access, within a different social network with an entirely different audience of users, on a web page or blog, on the open Web, and so on. This means that maintaining online privacy and security is not entirely an individual responsibility but one that is shared by an entire online community.

It's also important to realize that even if a social network privacy policy pledges that personal information will be kept private, there is a risk that it might be requested for official purposes, such as for legal investigations. As Marwick and associates (2010, 30) have explained, "Social network sites can be subpoenaed by a government agency to provide account information, even if that account is locked based on privacy settings." This broadens the population with potential access to personal information posted online from just the originator of the information to include that person's online friends, anyone to whom friends forward the information, employees of the company that hosts the social network, and even government agency employees. This is why a common rule of thumb for protecting online privacy and security is that users of social networks should post only information that they would be comfortable sharing with the general public. No matter how intimate the setting of a social network may seem, information posted there can quite easily become public and often does so without the poster's knowledge.

Cyberbullying: An Online Security Issue

In discussing youth and online security, the popular media have tended to focus on the dangers of sexual predators lurking in chat rooms and other online environments. In actuality, interactions between youth and these types of criminals are relatively rare (Hinduja and Patchin 2008), rarer even than in the offline world. Indeed, "The percentage of youth reporting dangerous offline contact as a result of online encounters is low, and Internet-initiated sexual assaults are rare" (Biegler and Boyd 2010, 5). As Biegler and Boyd have explained:

> Concerns about online predators are pervasive, but the image that most people hold doesn't necessarily match with the data about sexual crimes against minors. For starters, the emphasis on what takes place online tends to obscure the fact that most cases of sex crimes against children do not involve the Internet at all. (Biegler and Boyd 2010, 3)

A much more widespread threat to online security is online bullying, or "cyberbullying." As Siegle has explained, "The Internet and other technology-related devices are particularly suited to nonviolent types of bullying such as name-calling" (Siegle 2010, 14). Librarians can focus on educating teens about this lesser-known security risk to help them avoid emotionally (and sometimes physically) dangerous online interactions.

Just as the common activities that take place in online social networks are extensions of teens' face-to-face daily social interactions with peers and relatives, cyberbullying is an electronic extension of more traditional face-to-face bullying practices. Biegler and Boyd (2010) have stressed that teens who are likely to be targets of bullying in the offline world are similarly vulnerable in online environments:

> While the Internet has affected the contours of bullying and harassment, research continues to emphasize the interplay between what occurs online and what takes place offline. Many of the same youth are susceptible to victimization and those who engage in online bullying are not wholly distinct from those who bully offline. (Biegler and Boyd 2010, 4)

Biegler and Boyd have also cited research indicating that cyberbullying is less common than bullying in the offline world (Biegler and Boyd 2010, 10).

Nonetheless, cyberbullying does occur, and it is an important issue of concern to librarians and educators. Willard, of the Center for Safe and Responsible Use of the Internet, has defined cyberbullying as "being cruel to others by sending or posting harmful material or engaging in other forms of social aggression using the Internet or other digital technologies" (Willard 2007, 1). She identified eight types of cyberbullying:

1. *Flaming*, or engaging in arguments using angry and offensive language
2. *Harassment*, or sending repeated frightening and/or offensive communications
3. *Denigration*, or posting false information to try to damage a person's reputation or relationships
4. *Impersonation*, or pretending to be someone else online and causing mischief using the stolen identity
5. *Outing*, or revealing another person's secrets or embarrassing information online
6. *Trickery*, or tricking someone into revealing private information and then revealing it online
7. *Exclusion*, or deliberately excluding a person from an online group
8. *Cyberstalking*, or using online media to stalk and frighten someone (Willard 2007, 1–2)

Librarians can teach teens about these various types of cyberbullying, both in order to be able to recognize if they are its victims as well as to discourage them from becoming online bullies themselves. Educating teens about the potential emotional and physical damage that can result from such practices can go a long way toward helping teens to become safer users of online social networks and more responsible digital citizens.

Sexting: A Growing Threat to Privacy and Security

Although the chance of encountering sexual predators online is pretty slim, the likelihood of teens engaging in "sexting" (sex texting) is somewhat higher. Exact rates of sexting practices are not known, but it does seem to be a growing trend among teens. Sexting involves sending suggestive or nude pictures of oneself via text messaging. Librarians should explain to teens that once they send such an image, they no longer have control over it. An angry boyfriend or girlfriend can send it to thousands of other people or even post it online for the entire online world to see. These events are not only embarrassing but can lead to serious legal trouble. A number of state legislators are considering laws intended to reduce sexting by minors by making this practice a legal offense. For example, in June 2010, the Pennsylvania House of Representatives passed a law enabling district attorneys to charge minors with summary offenses or second-degree misdemeanors for sexting (Andren 2010, A1). And, of course, sending images of minors that go beyond being merely suggestive to being truly pornographic is already a federal offense. (See chapter 7 for a deeper discussion of the legal issues.)

Whether or not the Pennsylvania bill becomes law, the point here is that posting or texting risqué photos can have serious ramifications for teens' future lives. In his discussion of privacy in the age of the social Web, Notess (2006) concludes that "In general, the best privacy protection is to consider carefully the repercussions of posting anything that may possibly live online longer than we ourselves will." Librarians can help teens to become aware that information posted in social networks is not truly private, no matter how intimate the setting may seem to be. The companies that own social networks typically store information posted to them and—no matter what their privacy policies might claim—that information can be shared for legal purposes, as explained above. Thus, we need to teach teens not to post or text any potentially embarrassing or licentious content, even to close friends.

WHAT TEENS THINK ABOUT PRIVACY AND SECURITY IN SOCIAL NETWORKS

Keeping these issues in mind, let's look at what a group of real teens think about privacy and security in relation to social networking, and to texting via cell phones as well. We return now to the study of high school seniors discussed in chapter 2. In brief, the study involved interviewing 45 high school seniors using focus groups to learn about their mediated communication habits. Even though most of the teens were frequent and enthusiastic users of these tools, they did bring up a number of related concerns that were repeated throughout all six focus group sessions without the interview moderators prompting them to discuss their concerns. The teens often spoke about their worries related to online privacy and security throughout all six focus group interviews, indicating that they had given these issues considerable thought.

Views about Information Privacy and Social Networking

In terms of social networks, one reason for the overwhelming popularity of Facebook among these teens was the belief that it offered more privacy than other social networks. As one of the boys said: "Facebook is pretty private. You can make it pretty private." Another added that with Facebook "you get friend requests from people you actually know, but with MySpace, I just got random friend requests.... I didn't know any of them. I don't know anybody from South Dakota." And while the students knew they could refuse friend requests from strangers, they did not like the idea of strangers "watching" them online.

Although most of the 45 students thought that Facebook offered advanced privacy controls, many were unsure exactly how secure they were or how to implement them:

Student 1: I think there is a way you can make it where only your friends can see the pictures.

Student 2: You can make it where they can't see your page unless you add them as a friend.

Student 3: That doesn't make it private, though.

To these students, online safety was a learning process. When one of the boys joined Facebook a couple of years previously, for example, he created an open profile that enabled anyone to see his information. He had since become wary of letting strangers view his personal information and therefore changed his profile to a more restrictive setting. "You become more aware of those issues as you become a more experienced user," he explained. He had also added a lock on his cell phone so that no one could look at his stored text messages. "You learn your limits," he concluded. Other research backs up the idea that increased Internet experience is tied to a better understanding of online privacy issues. Simply put, teens who spend more time online tend to be more concerned with online privacy issues (Moscardelli and Devine 2007).

For these seniors, the most common method of protecting one's privacy within social networking communities was to limit their online friends to known individuals. Exceptions included friend requests from people with "at least five or six mutual friends" and requests from unknown students who indicated that they were planning to attend the same colleges after high school graduation.

Many of the students also limited family members' and other adults' access in order to protect their privacy:

Male student: My mom has a Facebook, and like a couple of my uncles do. I was their friend, but they can't know what is going on in my social life. So I deleted them. My mom gives me a friend request every once in a while, but I just reject it.

Moderator: Does she ask you about it?

Male student: She asks, but I will just be like, "No. You aren't going to be my friend on Facebook. I live in the same house as you."

Female student: Yeah. My dad was going to get a Facebook, and I convinced him not to get one.

Another one of the boys explained that trust and shared values dictated whether he would friend adults:

I am friends with one of my parents' friends on Facebook. I feel comfortable with her. I don't hide anything from her. But one of my aunts has different values than my family. So in my pictures, even if I am not doing anything bad, I don't want to portray my friends like that. I type in her name and don't let her see this album. I don't want to show my friends as bad kids.

Views about Information Security and Social Networking

Closely related to worries about online privacy were worries about online security. The study participants identified three types of security threats related to social network use: (1) threats to physical security, (2) threats to academic/vocational security, and (3) threats to emotional security.

First, the students thought of physical security threats in terms of unknown and potentially dangerous individuals gaining access to their personal data. They felt that this type of threat was especially present in social networking sites, perhaps reflecting the popular media's frequent portrayal of social networking sites as dangerous (Agosto and Abbas 2009; Hinduja and Patchin 2008).

Before friending an unfamiliar person, many of the teens described engaging in "Facebook stalking"—gathering as much information within Facebook as possible about another person without the other person's knowledge. Facebook stalking was not seen as a negative behavior but as a practical behavior both for security reasons and for assistance in determining whether or not to begin a relationship with a new person.

The students also used other methods for increasing their online security. Some of them had registered for Facebook accounts using pseudonyms to protect their online security. For example, one of the girls used only her first and middle names on Facebook for, as she explained: "privacy and safety. You just hear stories, and you would rather be safe than sorry." One of the boys in this same focus group session responded that he used just his first name with his last initial for the same reasons.

Many also expressed skepticism about revealing personal information online, again related to security concerns. For example:

Male student 1: People make [Facebook] groups when they break their [cell] phones.

Male student 2: People are like, "I need your numbers because I broke my phone." Who actually joins? That is kind of dangerous because people you don't know can get your numbers.

In addition to threats to physical security, the teens worried about threats to their academic/vocational security. They worried that school officials might find scandalous information online that could jeopardize their chances at being accepted to colleges. As one of the boys said, "I have heard of people getting rejected from colleges because they had seen their Facebook profiles. And pictures." The teens also worried that potential future employers might find negative information and images online and refuse to hire them, as "anything digital sticks around."

Additional security concerns included threats to emotional security, or the possibility that unknown persons could misrepresent them online. For example, two of the boys had had their MySpace accounts hacked. One was visibly upset as he told the story of a hacker posting a racist message on his profile to make it look as if he had posted it himself. He responded by getting "rid of my MySpace right there." He then switched his social networking home base to Facebook, which he perceived as safer. He attributed the recent decline in teen MySpace use to security flaws, saying: "A website like Facebook or MySpace can only survive if it has a reputation as being safe."

On the other hand, the students were familiar with ways to circumvent security controls, such as lying about their ages to create accounts. As one of the girls explained:

> I got my Facebook in eighth grade. And then our Catholic school found out about it, and they made us stop. They made us delete them. Because when you're on Facebook you are in a network, like [my high school] is on a network. But [my middle school] was on a network, so supposedly they could control it. They found certain pictures of things and got us in trouble for it. They made us delete them. But then I got a new one with a new name. There are ways around stuff like that.

Again, protecting online information privacy and security becomes a balancing act. Teens must learn to balance the need to share information with the need to make smart, safe online choices. This study also highlights the importance of educating teens to become intelligent, informed users, as in the case of the boy who described his learning to protect his privacy online as an ongoing process. Educating teens about how to become smarter, safer users of social networks and other information communication technologies is likely to be more helpful over the long term by teaching them lifelong survival skills rather than merely "protecting" teens from potentially harmful online information (such as filtering information or restricting social network access).

HOW LIBRARIANS CAN HELP TEENS PROTECT THEIR ONLINE PRIVACY AND SECURITY

This study has much to teach us about the role for librarians in helping teens to make smart, safe online choices. One of the most important ways that librarians can help teens to become safer users of social networks is to encourage them to read privacy policies and to help them choose appropriate privacy and security settings. As Marwick, Diaz, and Palfrey have explained, "It seems that many SNS [social networking sites] users do not understand or read privacy policies or settings" (Marwick et al. 2010, 29).

In teaching teens about online privacy and security issues, it's also important to teach them about the different types of cyberbullying discussed above, both to enable teens to protect themselves from becoming cyberbullying victims and to make them aware of the potential ramifications of engaging in cyberbullying themselves.

Willard has offered useful tips for designing cyberbullying awareness and prevention workshops. She suggests that:

> Students should be warned about the negative consequences of online retaliation and posting material that could be perceived as a threat. Students need specific guidelines on how to prevent and stop cyberbullying. Educating bystanders about the importance of speaking out, providing assistance to victims, and reporting concerns is important. (Willard 2007, 12)

She also stresses the importance of creating clear school policies against cyberbullying when using school computers. The same is true for public library computer use policies. (See chapter 7 for a discussion of acceptable use policies for library computers.)

To reduce other types of risky online encounters, such as encounters with online predators, another important recommendation is to encourage teens to communicate online with people they already know in the offline world. Schrock and Boyd (2008) have pointed out that security risks are much lower in communicating with friends and classmates than with strangers. Indeed, to reduce the possibility of interactions with sexual predators, many guidelines for parents and teachers suggest limiting youths' online friends to people they know in the offline world. While this might help to reduce such incidents, it ignores the fact that many risky sexual encounters that involve some form of online interaction occur with people youth know in the offline world prior to communicating with them online. It does, however, highlight the importance of teaching teens to consider possible security risks when deciding whom to friend within social networks.

Another way to approach educating teens to become safer social network users is to focus on common practices that put teens at risk of jeopardizing their online privacy and security. Tedeschi (2009) has identified five privacy and security mistakes that teens commonly make online: (1) broadcasting personal information to the entire Internet, (2) sharing passwords, (3) befriending strangers, (4) baring their souls, and (5) forgetting their futures. Libraries can help teens avoid these five types of mistakes by:

1. Teaching teens and their parents/guardians how to use social network privacy settings to limit who can access their personal information. Settings vary from social network to social network, as explained above, and they periodically change within each network as well. Librarians can offer classes to teach teens how to set up social network accounts, how to select the most restrictive privacy and security settings, and to learn how revisit their privacy and security settings on a periodic basis.

2. Explaining the possible consequences of sharing social network passwords (or any passwords, for that matter). Some teens think that sharing passwords is an act of friendship and intimacy. Teens need to understand that if an argument arises or if a relationship comes to an end, others can use their passwords to access their accounts and post defamatory, dishonest, or otherwise harmful information about them. To protect themselves, teens should never share their passwords with anyone other than trusted parents or guardians. Period. Librarians can also teach adolescents how to select passwords that are difficult for others to guess or to use computer programs to hack.

3. Talking with teens about the importance of limiting their online friends to people they know and trust in the offline world. Although it's unlikely that strangers wishing to friend a teen are sexual predators or other types of criminals, it is still a possibility. And even if strangers wishing to be friends are not sexual predators or other types of criminals, friending strangers frees up personal information for strangers to misuse. Strangers may repost personal information, such as personal photographs and personal stories, anywhere they wish, resulting in a risky loss of control over personal data. Strangers might also try to market unwanted

products and services to teens or to engage them in otherwise bothersome interactions.

4. Helping teens to understand that even though they can limit the people who have access to their online information, social networks are never fully private spaces. A good rule of thumb to teach teens about deciding what kinds of information to post online is to teach them to post only information that they would be comfortable making public, such as putting it on a poster in the school cafeteria. Baring one's soul and revealing private thoughts in a social network is risky, just as hanging a poster announcing one's personal thoughts in the school cafeteria might open one up to public teasing and ridicule. Librarians can help teens understand that even though social networks may appear to be private spaces, they are largely public in nature and should be thought of as public spaces.

5. Reminding teens that information posted online—even in jest— can last for decades. Today's crazy party picture might become embarrassing in 5 or 10 years (or even next week). It's also important to explain to teens that once it's put online, information can be nearly impossible to delete because others can pass it on and reuse it however they wish. Notess (2009) used the example of a teen posting a picture of himself with a group of his friends on his Facebook page: "What is to stop one of his friends from not only tagging himself but also copying the photo and uploading it to Flickr, Ning, MySpace, or another site?" Even if the first boy erases the photo off of his Facebook page, it may live on in other places without his knowledge or consent. (Chapter 7 continues this discussion on teaching teens to be good digital citizens and on the role that librarians can play by promoting and modeling legal and ethical technology practices.)

These various methods for increasing online privacy and security might seem obvious to us as information-savvy adults, but to many teens, they are not so obvious. Consequently, the most important way in which librarians can help to protect teens' online privacy and security is by talking with them about these very important issues and making them aware of the possible ramifications of their online behaviors.

WHERE TO GO FOR MORE INFORMATION

To learn more about online safety, the Federal Trade Commission's Division of Consumer and Business Education recommends the following websites (their URLs are listed under "Websites" at the end of this chapter):

- **OnGuardOnline.gov:** This is a federal government site that offers tips for online safety. It includes videos and interactive quizzes that can be used with teens in library computer safety workshops and classes.
- **ConnectSafely:** Created by the authors of the book *MySpace Unraveled: What It Is and How to Use It Safely* (Magid and Collier 2006), this site includes online safety information for kids and teens. Of particular interest is Social Web Tips for Teens, which lists suggestions for the safe use of social networks and other social media.
- **WiredSafety:** WiredSafety claims to be "the largest and oldest online safety, education, and help group in the world." It includes extensive links for librarians and educators as well as resources for kids, tweens, and teens.
- **CyberBully411:** Maintained by the nonprofit organization Internet Solutions for Kids, Inc., CyberBully411 includes information for children and teens interested in learning how to protect themselves from online harassment. It also provides a forum where youth who have experienced online harassment can share their stories.

CONCLUSION: MAXIMIZING BENEFITS, REDUCING RISK

Writing this chapter was especially difficult. We wanted to discuss the important issues of online privacy and security, but we also wanted to be careful not to exaggerate the dangers of online social networks and other forms of medicated communication. Yes, communicating online can be risky, but so can nearly every other common human activity. As librarians, we must be aware of the potential risks but not exaggerate them to the point that we deprive teens from partaking in this important part of modern culture and modern coming-of-age in the online world. As Biegler and Boyd have argued, it is counterproductive to:

> simply protect [youth] until their eighteenth birthday and then expect them to be responsible digital citizens.... The more that we can do to create channels of communication between youth and responsible adults and empower youth to play an active role in any intervention, the more successful we will be in combating the challenges we face with respect to risky behaviors and online safety. (Biegler and Boyd 2010, 4)

The many ideas presented throughout this chapter can help us to achieve this goal of working to educate teens about both the benefits and the risks of social networks, texting, and other forms of mediated communication. Our goal should be to educate teens—and their parents and guardians—and empower them to protect their own privacy and security as much as possible. In this way, we can help teens to garner the many benefits of social networking while minimizing the potential risks.

In chapter 7, Annette Lamb furthers our understanding of social networking as related to teens, as well as of online security and privacy issues, with a thoughtful discussion related to the rights and responsibilities of teens, the major federal laws in place or currently being considered, and the legal aspects of using social networks with teens that librarians need to consider before implementing social networks within their libraries.

REFERENCES

Agosto, Denise E., and June Abbas. "Teens and Social Networking: How Public Libraries Are Responding to the Latest Online Trend." *Public Libraries* 48 (2009): 32–37.

Andren. Kari. "Pennsylvania House Approves Plan to Make 'Sexting' a Crime." *The Patriot News,* June 30, 2010: A01.

BBC News. "Facebook Mulls U-turn on Privacy," http://www.time.com/time/business/article/0,8599,1990582,00.html (accessed May 19, 2010).

Biegler, Samantha, and Danah Boyd. "Risky Behaviors and Online Safety: A 2010 Literature Review," http://www.zephoria.org/files/2010SafetyLitReview.pdf (accessed July 10, 2010).

Fletcher, Dan. "How Facebook Is Redefining Privacy." *Time* (May 31, 2010): 175, http://www.time.com/time/business/article/0,8599,1990582,00.html/ (accessed May 31, 2010).

Havenstein, Heather. "Millennials Demand Changes in IT Strategy." *Computerworld* 42 (September 22, 2008): 12–13.

Hinduja, Sameer, and Justin W. Patchin. "Personal Information of Adolescents on the Internet: A Quantitative Analysis of MySpace." *Journal of Adolescence* 31 (2008): 125–46.

Hoofnagle, Chris, Jennifer King, Su Li, and Joseph Turow. "How Different Are Young Adults from Older Adults When It Comes to Information Privacy Attitudes and Policies?" April 14, 2010, http://papers.ssrn.com/sol3/papers.cfm?abstract_id=1589864/ (accessed July 11, 2010).

Lohr, Steve. "How Privacy Vanishes Online." *New York Times,* March 17, 2010: A1.

Magid, Larry, and Anne Collier. *MySpace Unraveled: What It Is and How to Use It Safely.* Berkeley, CA: Peachpit Press, 2006.

Marwick, Alice E., Diego Murgia Diaz, and John Palfrey. *Youth, Privacy and Reputation.* Cambridge, MA: Berkman Center for Internet & Society, 2010, http://cyber.law.harvard.edu/publications/2010/Youth_Privacy_Reputation_Lit_Review/ (accessed July 17, 2010).

Moscardelli, Deborah M., and Catherine Liston-Heyes. "Teens Surfing the Net: How Do They Learn to Protect Their Privacy?" *Journal of Business and Economics Research* 2 (2004): 43–56.

Moscardelli, Deborah M., and Richard Devine. "Adolescents' Concern for Privacy When Using the Internet: An Empirical Analysis of Predictors and Relationships with Privacy-Protecting Behaviors." *Family and Consumer Sciences Research Journal* 35 (March 2007): 232–52.

Notess, Greg R. "Privacy in the Age of the Social Web." *Online* 33 (July/August 2009): 41–43.

Schrock, Andrew, and Danah Boyd. "Online Threats to Youth: Solicitation, Harassment, and Problematic Content." Research Advisory Board Report for the Internet Safety Technical Task Force, 2008, http://www.danah.org/papers/ISTTF-RABLitReview.pdf/ (accessed May 31, 2010).

Siegle, Del. "Cyberbullying and Sexting: Technology Abuses of the 21st Century." *Gifted Child Today* 32 (2010): 14–18.

Tedeschi, Bob. "5 Mistakes (Even Smart) Kids Make Online." *Good Housekeeping* 249 (August 2009): 107.

Willard, Nancy. "Educator's Guide to Cyberbullying and Cyberthreats." Center for Safe and Responsible Use of the Internet. April 2007. http://www.cyberbully.org/cyberbully/docs/cbcteducator.pdf/ (accessed July 10, 2010).

Wortham, Jenna. "Facebook Glitch Brings New Privacy Worries." *New York Times* (May 5, 2010): 81.

WEBSITES

ConnectSafely, http://www.connectsafely.org/

CyberBully411, http://cyberbully411.org/

Federal Trade Commission, Division of Consumer and Business Education, http://www.ftc.gov/bcp/bcpocbe.shtm/

Internet Solutions for Kids, Inc., http://is4k.com/

OnGuardOnline.gov, http://www.onguardonline.gov/

Social Web Tips for Teens, http://www.connectsafely.org/Safety-Tips/social-web-tips-for-teens.html/

WiredSafety, http://www.wiredsafety.org/

WiredSafety for educators, http://wiredsafety.org/educators.html/

WiredSafety for youth, http://wiredsafety.org/youth.html/

◇ ◇ ◇

7

SOCIAL NETWORKING: TEEN RIGHTS, RESPONSIBILITIES, AND LEGAL ISSUES

Annette Lamb

Over the past several years, legislation has focused increasingly on the use of social technology by young people. In addition, many existing laws and federal regulations have been adapted and applied to the online environment. As a result, in using social networks, today's teens face ethical dilemmas as well as legal concerns.

In a 2009 MTV digital media use poll, more than 75% of young people aged 13 to 24 indicated that they had used a social network during the previous week, and 66% said that they had sent or received messages on MySpace, Facebook, or other social networks (MTV-AP 2009). Another recent study indicated that over 50% of all teens check social networking sites more than once daily (Common Sense Media 2009).

However, many teens haven't thought about the legal aspects of social network use. According to the MTV-AP study, more than half of young people stated that they had never thought about the risk of getting into trouble with the police for their social networking activities (MTV-AP 2009). This chapter describes the rights and responsibilities of teens, summarizes the major federal laws, and outlines what librarians need to know about the legal aspects of using social networks with teens in order to implement social networks within their libraries.

RIGHTS AND RESPONSIBILITIES

Rather than creating a culture of fear by focusing on the negative aspects of social networks and the law, we should design educational programs that stress the rights and responsibilities of Internet use. Teens need to learn how to make good choices in social networking situations, and both public and school librarians can teach teens about making good choices online.

Minors have the First Amendment right to access information for personal knowledge and to interact with their friends online. Access to technology tools such as social networks to share their thoughts is part of this right. In a school library setting, administrators may channel access based on academic needs. In a public library setting, the availability of social technology is important because no other access may be available for some teens.

In 2009, the American Library Association adopted the "Minors and Internet Interactivity: An Interpretation of the Library Bill of Rights" (American Library Association 2009, 1) document to protect and promote the rights of young people. This document states that "the rights of minors to retrieve, interact with, and create information posted on the Internet in schools and libraries are extensions of their First Amendment rights." The document notes that the use of social networks "poses two competing intellectual freedom issues—the protection of minors' privacy and the right of free speech" (American Library Association 2009, 1). Both privacy and intellectual freedom are discussed in this chapter.

Minors, the Internet, and the Law

Over the past decade, a number of laws have specifically addressed the use of the Internet by minors. In designing technology-enhanced library programs for young people, it's important to adhere to these laws and regulations.

Many bills related to minors and their use of social networks have been introduced. However, only a few have become law at the national level. The Electronic Privacy Information Center (EPIC) tracks bills related to privacy, speech, and cyberlibraries that are particularly useful for librarians. A number of the major laws that it tracks are described and updated below.

Child Pornography Prevention Act (CPPA) (18 U.S.C. § 2251)

This 1996 law, which expands the definition of child pornography to include "virtual child pornography" and "morphed" child pornography, prohibited a wide range of digital pornography. In a 2002 U.S. Supreme Court decision (*Ashcroft v. Free Speech Coalition* 2002), parts of this law were overturned. For instance, nonobscene images of teenagers engaging in sexual activity are now legal. Also, computer-generated images that do not link the creation of an image to child abuse are legal. Because the law applies to creators of images, it does not affect libraries directly. However, it does apply to young people who might create and share images on social networks.

Child Online Protection Act (COPA) (47 U.S.C. § 609)

This 1998 law prohibited the transmission of materials deemed "harmful to minors." It also restricted children under 13 from having accounts on some websites and required parental consent on others. It was passed more than a decade ago, but as of the year 2009 it had not taken effect because U.S. federal courts had ruled that it violated the constitutional protection of free speech. In 2009, the U.S. Supreme Court refused to hear appeals, which continued to prevent COPA from being applied.

Children's Internet Protection Act (CIPA) (20 U.S.C. § 6301)

Established in 2000, this law states that "schools and libraries that have computers with Internet access must certify that they have in place certain Internet safety policies and technology protection measures in order...to receive discounted Internet access, Internet services, and internal connection services" (Children's Internet Protection Act 2001, 19394). In other words, filters must be in place to block objectionable materials. However, the act also states that it's up to individual schools and libraries to determine the best approach to filtering and to choose those measures and policies that are most appropriate for their communities. The statute defines a minor as anyone who has not attained the age of 17.

Broadband Data Improvement Act (BDIA) (47 U.S.C. § 1301)

This 2008 federal law states that districts receiving federal funding must be "educating minors about appropriate online behavior, including interacting with other individuals on social network websites and in chat rooms and cyberbullying awareness and response" (Broadband Data Improvement Act 2008, 9). This law has a direct impact on school and public libraries that rely on federal funding.

E-Rate Requirements

E-Rate is the common name for the Universal Service Fund, which was created as a part of the Telecommunications Act of 1996 (47 U.S.C. § 609). E-Rate is a federal program that provides discounts on Internet access and/or internal connection services as well as other technology. For many schools and libraries, the requirements of E-Rate also impact technology programs, as it requires compliance with laws including CIPA and BDIA.

Terms-of-Service Contract (ToS)

Can a 14-year-old student register for a Second Life account? What happens to photographs teens share on Flickr? Are middle school students allowed to set up Facebook groups? These questions can be answered by examining the ToS provided on a social networking site. These contracts are not laws but policies of individual websites and other social network utilities. Librarians should examine these documents carefully before using social networking sites to promote their services and programs. Teens should also be encouraged to read the ToS of each website before creating an account. Unfortunately, some service agreements are difficult to understand, and some contradict their published missions. For instance, Google encourages educators and librarians to use Google Apps with teens. However, Google's ToS states that a person may not use the service if he or she is "not of legal age to form a binding contract," which in most cases means at least 18 years of age.

In addition to these various laws and policies, many commercial websites, including social networks, continue to limit membership on the basis of age. Each website determines rules such as age restrictions, who maintains ownership of content, and how the site is administered. These rules are designed to protect the website owners as well as to inform users. Further, most social networks require that users agree to a contract in setting up a new account. This contract is sometimes called a statement of rights and responsibilities. Agreements such as these are legally binding contracts, and breach of a contract has possible legal implications. Generally a violator's account is simply terminated and he or she is told not to reregister.

Intellectual Freedom

Related to the concept of laws and policies governing youths' use of Internet resources is the concept of intellectual freedom. Intellectual freedom is the right of individuals to seek and receive information from all points of view, as well as to express ideas and information with almost no restrictions. In the United States, the concepts of intellectual freedom and freedom of expression are based in the First Amendment of the Bill of Rights of the U.S. Constitution. Freedom of expression is a human right that encompasses freedom of speech. Libraries and librarians should protect and promote this right including the use of social networks. Balance is needed between the rights of young people to access information and the wishes of teachers and parents to protect their children from harm. These laws were designed to protect intellectual freedom as well as the needs of youth. Related laws and online practices are described below.

First Amendment Rights

The First Amendment to the U.S. Constitution is part of the Bill of Rights and gives citizens the right to access information and participate in discussions available through social technology. This right applies to young people as well as adults. Libraries serve an essential function in our society by providing access to computers that can be used by children and teenagers who may or may not have access to technology otherwise.

CIPA and Filtering

As explained above, the Children's Internet Protection Act (CIPA) requires that schools and libraries use filters to block access to visual depictions deemed obscene, to block child pornography, and to block materials harmful to minors. Unfortunately the default settings on most filter systems block many more Internet resources. Although it's important to meet the requirements of the law, librarians need to be aware that rigorous filters may be restricting student access to information. For instance, some filters block entire categories of websites, such as social networks.

Social Networks and Activism

Many young people are using social networks to become socially and politically active citizens and as a venue for freedom of expression. As such, social networks serve as an important platform for free speech. More than half of teens have joined an online community or group in support of a cause (Common Sense Media 2009). From joining causes featured on Facebook that are related to environmental issues to posting messages endorsing political candidates, teens use social networks to speak out on issues and support political campaigns.

Free Speech Cases

An increasing number of court cases have addressed the free speech rights of teens using social networks. From criticizing a principal over a school policy on body piercing to complaining about teaching practices, most courts have upheld the right of teens to speak freely online. However, some teens are unaware of the potential consequences of their actions. Some 46% of young people haven't thought about the risk of getting into trouble at school or with a boss for information posted on a social network (MTV-AP 2009). It falls to public and school librarians to educate teens about these possible consequences.

Harassment, Hate Speech, and Cyberbullying

Freedom of speech is not always a beneficial right. Sexual remarks, ridicule, and racial slurs are common on social networks. A recent survey by Common Sense Media (2009) found that 54% of teens had used social networking sites to complain about or make fun of teachers, 39% had posted something they later regretted, and 37% had made fun of other students. Librarians should help teens to be aware of the possible harms of negative speech online, including harassment.

Harassment includes a wide range of offensive behaviors intended to upset, disturb, or threaten. Cyberbullying is a specific type of harassment that occurs when a "a child, preteen, or teen is tormented, threatened, harassed, humiliated, embarrassed or otherwise targeted by another child, preteen or teen using Internet, interactive and digital technologies or mobile phones." Cyberbullying is being taken seriously by the court system. A teen in Britain was even jailed for posting death threats on Facebook (Salkeld 2009).

A number of organizations are dedicated to eliminating cyberbullying. They provide some useful information and resources for librarians. They include the following, and their websites are listed at the end of this chapter.

- National Crime Prevention Council
- STOP cyberbullying
- Cyberbullying Research Center

Online Bias and Hate Crimes

Along with cyberbullying, young people may also become involved in activities that involve bias-motivated online activities or hate crimes. Victims may be targeted based on race, religion, political affiliation, ethnicity, nationality, or age. In 2009, the Matthew Shepard Act (Pub. L. 111–84) added gender, gender identity, sexual orientation, and disability to the federal definition of hate crimes. These crimes are serious and can result in felony convictions.

Free Speech and Personal Responsibility

A fine line can be drawn between defamation laws, which are intended to protect people from harmful speech, and the right to freedom of speech. Individuals must be protected against reckless and unfounded allegations, so freedom of speech may be restricted to protect the reputations and rights of others. Teens need to understand that while censorship limits freedom, individuals must act responsibly. For example, the freedom of speech doesn't permit teens to make false statements about a principal or share altered images that may defame a former girlfriend. In a practice known as cybervetting, many businesses now evaluate the social network presence of potential employees (Berkelaar 2008). Some colleges even check social networks before admitting students to their programs (Lipka 2009), so teens need to be aware of the possible broader implications of irresponsible online behaviors.

Honesty and the Law

Although American citizens have the right to freedom of speech, they are also legally responsible for their words and actions. From texting white lies to impersonating a teacher online, some teens are using the anonymity of the Internet to avoid face-to-face encounters and in some cases to conduct illegal activity, including libel and fraud.

It's easy for teens to hide behind their Web pseudonyms without realizing that their actions extend to real life. Some 26% of teens have pretended to be someone else online, 18% have pretended to be an adult while chatting with someone online, and 16% have posted false information or lies about other people (Common Sense Media 2009).

Deceptive activities such as these may seem harmless to some teens. However, they can easily lead to serious consequences. For instance, using a stolen password to access a friend's social network account is not only dishonest but also an activity that breaks the ToS contract of most services and could lead to fraud charges.

Dishonesty

It's not uncommon for young people to lie or share false information on social networks. For instance, many preteens lie about their age to avoid age restrictions associated with social networking sites. A study titled "Teens, Privacy, and Online Social Networks" (Lenhart and Madden 2007) reported that 56% of teens posted fake information on their online profiles.

Libel

Libel is a written or otherwise published statement that unjustly conveys an unfavorable impression about someone. Many teens have experienced libelous behavior on social networks. According to the MTV-AP Digital Abuse poll (MTV-AP 2009), nearly 25% of young people found that someone had written something about them on the Internet that wasn't true. Teens may use social networks to vilify a former boyfriend or complain about a teacher, for example. These statements become calumnious when the claims are false and are published in a public manner, as on a social network. However, because a social network is more like a conversation than a published article, some people have called this type of crime slander because of its transitory nature. Regardless of the form, defamation is illegal. Additional examples involve accusing someone of a crime, alleging that someone has a disease, adversely reflecting on a person's fitness, or imputing serious sexual misconduct.

Fraud and Identity Theft

From identity theft to harmful hoaxes, fraud involves intentional deception for the purpose of personal gain or to damage to another person. Identity theft involves pretending to be someone else for some personal benefit. The Federal Computer Fraud and Abuse Act of 1986 (18 U.S.C. § 1001) has been applied to cybercrimes such as a woman who created a fake profile for the purpose of cyberbullying (Kravitz 2008). According to the MTV-AP Digital Abuse poll (MTV-AP 2009), 6% of young people have experienced someone impersonating them by creating a fake social network profile. Schools are taking this type of impersonation seriously. For instance, an eighth-grader in Pennsylvania was suspended for creating a fake profile depicting her principal in a negative light, and the suspension held up in court (Slater 2008).

Reporting Illegal Activity

Most teens seem to be willing to take action in dealing with dishonest and illegal activities. The vast majority of young people state that they would report someone else's inappropriate or illegal activities; 96% would sometimes or always report when someone was doing something against the law (MTV-AP 2009). Librarians can teach teens about the importance of reporting illegal and dangerous online behaviors.

Honesty and the Library

Although lying, spying, and harsh words are common teen behaviors online, librarians need to be aware of the legal ramifications particularly when library computers are used to access social networks. For instance, it's possible that a librarian could be subpoenaed to testify about whether a patron was using a particular computer at a specific time. Or a library director could be asked for physical records related to computer use.

Intellectual Property and the Copyright Law

While honesty can be an issue associated with copyright, a more common problem is misunderstanding of the laws associated with use of intellectual property.

Intellectual Property and Issues of Ownership

Teens who have written a poem, created a work of art, or composed a song have all created intellectual property. Half of teens have posted creative writing, artwork, videos, or music they created (Common Sense Media 2009). With so many students sharing their work online, it's important for them to understand their ownership rights to the items they create. When users agree to accept the Terms of Service agreement, they may be giving up their right to text, images, audio, and video that are shared on the network. It's therefore important to read the agreement before sharing intellectual property on a social network.

Copyright Law

Copyright law is intended to protect the rights of content developers and describes restrictions that can be placed on copying materials. In other words, if teens create information, they should get credit for it. This credit may take the form of an attribution line or a monetary payment. Teens must also be careful not to share materials copyrighted by others without first securing copyright clearance. Copyright infringement is a particular problem on social networks where sharing of images, audio content, and videos is easy, and many users lack knowledge of copyright laws and regulations.

Copyleft Approach

In contrast to copyright, copyleft describes the removal of restrictions on the use of ideas and information. People who wish to share their materials can use the copyleft license to allow others to reproduce, adapt, and distribute copies of their work. Rather than placing materials in the public domain without restriction, copyleft groups such as Creative Commons and GNU General Public License provide a range of flexible copyright protections for creative works. This approach is becoming increasingly popular in social network environments. For instance, Flickr encourages users to designate a Creative Commons license for images, and Swivel does the same for shared data.

Teens, Derivative Works, and Social Networks

According to Jackson (2008, 1), teens are among the most active creative producers of online content. "Online, esteem comes from recognition and peer validation. For young artists and entrepreneurs the potential for rapid, widespread attention is paramount." Increasingly, young people are involved in creating remixes and mash-ups using images, sounds, and videos from existing content. These are known as derivative works. Jackson (2008, 1) notes that "today's most-watched YouTube videos can spawn legions of offspring that include parodies, homages, and critiques. Teens also are active commentators, posting on blogs and forums in subject areas ranging from health and news to sports, entertainment, and politics." As a result, young people need to be aware of the situations where they are free to share their creations, when citations are required, and when sharing would be illegal.

Privacy Expectations and the Law

Privacy is another topic related to the legal issues surrounding teens and online social networking. Teens have the right to privacy. However, some young people lack the skills and dispositions to protect their personal information adequately. They must learn to differentiate between information about themselves that they should protect and the kinds of information that can be safely shared on social networks.

Protecting the privacy of peers must also be considered. Some 12% of young adults have experienced someone impersonating them or spying on them as they logged in on a social network (MTV-AP 2009).

The 1974 Family Educational Rights and Privacy Act (FERPA) (20 U.S.C. § 1221) protects the privacy of student education records including information stored on computers. However, this federal law allows schools to disclose those records to comply with parental and legal requests. Just as a teen's locker can be searched, a social networking site can be monitored if there is reasonable suspicion of misconduct.

The Fourth Amendment

The Fourth Amendment to the U.S. Constitution guards against unreasonable search and seizure, thereby protecting the privacy of citizens. In the article "The Fourth Amendment and Privacy Issues on the 'New' Internet: Facebook.com and MySpace.com," Hodge (2006, 123) identifies legal issues related to privacy expectations in social networks where users volunteer to share personal information with others through profiles and informational postings. Hodge states that "whether a person has a reasonable expectation of privacy is difficult to determine, but most people are not willing to give up all protection merely by signing online."

Privacy Expectations

While a person may have a subjective expectation of privacy on a social network, this may not be reasonable based on the openness of a network that involves friends of friends. Hodge (2006) uses the analogy of a safety deposit box at a bank to describe how information is stored in a social network. Individuals are provided with a storage space along with a key allowing them to share their space with others who have the key, or a password in the case of cyberspace. Librarians can use similar analogies to teach teens that their privacy online is not as secure as they might think.

Images and Privacy

According to the MTV digital media use poll, 81% of young adults possess a cell phone with a camera. Not surprisingly, 89% of young people would be somewhat or very much upset if someone posted nude photos or videos of them on a social network. However, 10% of young people have digitally transmitted nude photos of themselves to someone else, and these photos could easily be posted on a social network. Indeed, 11% of young people have experienced someone putting embarrassing pictures or videos of themselves on a web page without their permission (MTV-AP 2009).

Sexting

Teens are increasingly involved in "sexting" activities such as sending nude, sexually explicit, or suggestive images. These images sometimes wind up on social networking sites. As many as 44% of young adults feel that sharing nude photos of people their age is a very serious problem (MTV-AP 2009). Teens need to understand that taking, transmitting, and even possessing naked images of a minor is a federal offense, and the consequences of these behaviors can be serious. A high school senior who shares suggestive images of a freshman girlfriend or boyfriend could even end up with a felony conviction.

Blackmail

Of young adults participating in the MTV poll, 65% stated that they would be very upset if someone threatened to post negative content on social networking sites or tell other people private things (true or untrue), if he or she didn't do as they demanded (MTV-AP 2009). About 8% of young people reported that this type of blackmail has happened to them (MTV-AP 2009). Blackmail is illegal and young people need to be aware that there are laws to protect them from online blackmail.

BALANCING PRIVACY AND SOCIALIZING

The good news is that a majority of teens are aware of the need for online privacy. A study from the Pew Internet & American Life Project found that "the majority of teens actively manage their online profiles to keep the information they believe is most sensitive away from the unwanted gaze of strangers, parents and other adults" (Lenhart and Madden 2007, 1). Teens need to be aware of what constitutes invasion of privacy in social networking situations. For instance, public disclosure of private facts a reasonable person would find objectionable is not appropriate in a social networking environment that is open to friends of friends. False light privacy is the damage to a person's mental or emotional well-being based on disclosing information that may or may not be true about their personal life. For instance, a teen might comment on a peer's photo that she looks pregnant. The comment may be made with malice or in jest; however, it's sometimes difficult to tell in a social situation. Any statements that could be considered an invasion of privacy or that might shed false light on an individual can be harmful regardless of the intent.

Safety Issues

Many librarians, educators, and parents have expressed legitimate concerns about the safety of teens online. Nancy Willard (2006), director of the Center for Safe and Responsible Internet Use, has identified three concerns. First, brain research studies reveal that teens have immature frontal lobe development, making consistent, well-reasoned decisions difficult. In other words, teens can make poor choices in social situations. Second, many parents do not pay sufficient attention to the online activities of their teens. Third, dangerous adults are attracted to environments where young people make poor choices and lack supervision.

When teens share personal information, they become susceptible to business spammers, identity theft, and sexual predators. However, a recent study titled "Enhancing Child Safety and Online Technologies" (Berkman Center for Internet & Society 2008) found that online risk has been present throughout the history of the Internet and that only a tiny minority of youth are susceptible to sexual exploitation resulting from their online activities. The authors concluded that online bullying and harassment are the most common risks for teens.

Risks

Although many social networks, such as Facebook, claim to deny accounts to sex offenders, it's difficult for the social networks to monitor new users closely. In a 2009 report for the Crimes Against Children Research Center, Wolak and colleagues (2009, 2) found that sex offenses against youth have declined and that Internet-initiated crimes constituted only 1% of overall child sexual exploitation. They concluded that "there was no evidence that online predators were stalking or abducting unsuspecting victims based on information they posted at social networking sites." However, some teens do become victims in social networking settings. In one study, 18% of teens indicated that someone had posted humiliating photos of them, and 19% said that they had been harassed or cyberbullied (Common Sense Media 2009).

ORGANIZATIONS THAT SPECIALIZE IN ONLINE SAFETY EDUCATION

Many organizations provide materials to assist librarians in teaching young people to be safe when using social networks. These include the following (their websites are listed at the end of this chapter):

- Connect Safely
- GetNetWise

- IKeepSafe
- iSafe
- NetSmartz
- WebWiseKids
- Wired Safety

ACCEPTABLE USE POLICIES

Next, given ongoing changes in legislation as well as the importance of establishing clear guidelines for users, an up-to-date Acceptable Use Policy (AUP) is essential for school and public libraries. AUPs tell library users how they can and cannot use the library's computer resources, and they explain any consequences of unapproved use. The AUP should include guidelines for permissible behavior when using library technology and also state consequences for inappropriate activities. The AUP may also include the library's internet safety policy, as required by the CIPA.

AUP Maintenance

Regularly updating the AUP provides an opportunity for librarians to keep current on new legislation as well as to consider the role of new technologies. Rather than designing a policy focusing on negative statements such as "don't do this" or "that's not allowed," librarians should consider an approach that stresses intellectual freedom, safe behavior, and social responsibility. Although the AUP may be used to support sanctions for irresponsible behavior, this proactive approach can also serve as a tool for encouraging positive use of technology. ALA's "Minors and Internet Inter-activity: An Interpretation of the Library Bill of Rights" reminds librarians that "instances of inappropriate use of such academic tools should be addressed as individual behavior issues, not as justification for restricting or banning access to interactive technology" (American Library Association 2009).

School and Library Liability

In school settings, AUPs are intended to protect students, educators, and the school district. However, when the school's network is used to engage in illegal activities, liability concerns may be raised. Whether a librarian has observed cyberbullying activities, tolerated racial hostilities on a social network, or overheard a threat to post inappropriate images on a social network, he or she is responsible for reporting activities that may cause physical or emotional injury. If a teen is injured and the situation should have been foreseen, the educator, librarian, and school can be found negligent.

DIGITAL CITIZENSHIP

Today's teens can be considered digital citizens, and it's essential that today's librarians promote and model legal and ethical technology practices. Educating young people about their rights and responsibilities as digital citizens is also a requirement of some legislation. For instance, the Broadband Data Improvement Act: Protecting Children in the 21st Century (2008) amended CIPA to require schools to teach minors about ethical online behavior. According to the MTV-AP Digital Abuse (MTV-AP 2009) survey, more than 75% of young people think digital abuse such as harassing, impersonating, or embarrassing others online is a serious problem, and 34% feel that it affects them personally.

Approaches to Teaching Digital Citizenship

An increasing number of online resources are available for helping young people deal with topics related to digital citizenship. These include the following (their websites are listed at the end of this chapter):

- Common Sense Media
- CyberSmart
- Digital Citizenship
- Digizen
- A Thin Line

Promoting Ethical Online Behavior

Ethical behavior is a crucial part of good digital citizenship. Librarians can promote ethical behavior a number of ways:

- **By modeling effective use.** Use social networks to model appropriate uses of the technology. Post book trailers on YouTube, use Facebook to share library activities, and share images from library events on Flickr.

- **By engaging teens.** Use social networks to promote traditional services and resources, offer virtual programs, and provide news and information.
- **By being available.** Use social networks to increase your visibility. Participate in online discussions, virtual book clubs, and chat with teens.
- **By building communities.** Use social networks to create a sense of community through book clubs, virtual experiences, and online workshops.
- **By sponsoring events.** Design, develop, and offer programs that place an emphasis on ethical online behavior. Demonstrate how public domain images can be used in remixes, and encourage students to compose and share original images, music, and videos.

AASL STANDARDS

The American Association of School Librarians (AASL) has developed Standards for the 21st-Century Learner that include skills, dispositions, and responsibilities essential for today's digital citizens (American Association of School Librarians 2007). The first set of these standards states that teens must learn to access and evaluate the information found on social networks.

- Standard 1.1.5: Evaluate information found in selected sources on the basis of accuracy, validity, appropriateness for needs, importance, and social and cultural context.
- Standard 4.1.7: Use social networks and information tools to gather and share information.
- Standard 4.4.4: Interpret new information based on cultural and social context.
- Standard 2.3.3: Use valid information and reasoned conclusions to make ethical decisions.

A subset of these standards relates to ethical and legal behavior on social networks. That is, teens must learn to follow legal regulations and demonstrate ethical behavior associated with social networks.

- Standard 1.3.3: Follow ethical and legal guidelines in gathering and using information.
- Standard 3.1.6: Use information and technology ethically and responsibly.

- Standard 3.1.2: Participate and collaborate as members of a social and intellectual network of learners.
- Standard 3.2.2: Show social responsibility by participating actively with others in learning situations and by contributing questions and ideas during group discussions.
- Standard 4.3.1: Participate in the social exchange of ideas, both electronically and in person.
- Standard 4.3.4: Practice safe and ethical behaviors in personal electronic communication and interaction.[1]

In addition to developing stand-alone instructional materials to address these standards, it's important for school librarians to weave these learning outcomes throughout the curriculum. For instance, the school librarian and middle school social studies teachers might collaborate on an activity that uses social technology within the context of a current issues lesson.

Public librarians can support these standards through modeling effective uses of social media in programs such as virtual book clubs. They can also build tutorials, produce brochures, and promote family programs that involve parents and teens in meaningful discussions about social networking. Chapter 8 explains how to create these programs and resources.

CONCLUSION

From YouTube and Flickr to Facebook and MySpace, social networks and social media are playing an increasingly important role in the lives of teens. However, many young people are not aware of the legal and ethical ramifications of their online activities. Teens need to be aware that illegal and inappropriate behavior can happen in social networking situations. As librarians, we have an obligation to ensure that young people become responsible digital citizens. However, rather than overemphasizing the negative aspects of social networking, public and school librarians should consider an approach that focuses on practical suggestions for handling tough situations and on the many positive applications of online communication and collaboration.

NOTE

1. Excerpted from *Standards for the 21st-Century Learner* by the American Association of School Librarians, a division of the American Library Association, copyright © 2007 American Library Association. Available for download at www.ala.org/aasl/standards. Used with permission.

REFERENCES

American Association of School Librarians. "Standards for the 21st Century Learner" (2007), http://www.ala.org/aasl/standards/ (accessed January 8, 2009).

American Library Association. "Minors and Internet Interactivity: An Interpretation of the Library Bill of Rights" (July 15, 2009), http://www.ala.org/ala/aboutala/offices/oif/statementspols/statementsif/interpretations/minorsinternetinteractivity.cfm/ (accessed December 15, 2009).

Ashcroft v. Free Speech Coalition, 535 U.S. 234 (2002) 198 F.3d 1083, affirmed, http://supct.law.cornell.edu/supct/html/00–795.ZS.html/ (accessed December 15, 2009).

Berkelaar, Brenda. "Cybervetting (Potential) Employees: An Emerging Area of Study for Organizational Communication." Paper presented at the Annual Meeting of the International Communication Association, Montreal, Quebec, Canada, May 22, 2008, http://www.allacademic.com/meta/p234515_index.html/ (accessed January 8, 2010).

Berkman Center for Internet & Society. "Enhancing Child Safety and Online Technologies." (2008). http://cyber.law.harvard.edu/pubrelease/isttf/ (accessed December 15, 2009).

Broadband Data Improvement Act. (October 2, 2008), http://www.govtrack.us/data/us/bills.text/110/s/s1492enr.pdf/ (accessed December 15, 2009).

Children's Internet Protection Act. *Federal Register* 66, no. 73 (April 16, 2001): 19394–98.

Common Sense Media. "Is Technology Changing Childhood? A National Poll on Teens and Social Networking," http://www.commonsensemedia.org/teen-social-media/ (accessed December 15, 2009).

Hodge, Matthew J. "The Fourth Amendment and Privacy Issues on the 'New' Internet: Facebook.com and MySpace.com." *Southern Illinois University Law Journal* 31 (2006): 95–123. http://www.law.siu.edu/research/31fallpdf/fourthamendment.pdf/ (accessed December 15, 2009).

Jackson, Graziella. "Dot Teen: Portrait of a Facebook Generation." *Insight* (April 2008), http://www.navigationarts.com/insight/teen_internet_use/ (accessed December 15, 2009).

Kravitz, Derek. "MySpace Suicide Case Expands Web Law." *Washington Post* (November 28, 2008), http://voices.washingtonpost.com/washingtonpost investigations/2008/11/myspace_suicide_ruling_a_water.html/ (accessed January 8, 2009).

Lenhart, Amanda, and Madden, Mary. "Teens, Privacy and Online Social Networks." Pew Internet &American Life Project (April 2007), http://www.pewinternet.org/~/media//Files/Reports/2007/PIP_Teens_Privacy_SNS_Report_Final.pdf.pdf/ (accessed December 15, 2009).

Lipka, Sara. "Social Media in Admissions: No Longer a Choice." *The Chronicle of Higher Education* (April 29, 2009), http://chronicle.com/blogPost/Social-Media-in-Admissions-No/4655/ (accessed January 8, 2010).

MTV-AP. "MTV-AP Digital Abuse Study." Knowledge Works (September 23, 2009), http://surveys.ap.org/data%5CKnowledgeNetworks%5CAP_Digital_Abuse_Topline_092209.pdf/ (accessed December 15, 2009).

Salkeld, Luke. "First Cyberbully Jailed After Facebook Death Threats." *Mail Online* (August 21, 2009), http://www.dailymail.co.uk/news/article-1208147/First-cyberbully-jailed-Facebook-death-threats.html/ (accessed January 8, 2009).

Slater, Dan. "Cyberbullying & the Law: Free Speech's Next Frontier." *Wall Street Journal* Law Blog (December 11, 2008), http://blogs.wsj.com/law/2008/12/11/cyberbullying-the-law-free-speechs-next-frontier/ (accessed January 8, 2009).

Willard, Nancy E. "A Briefing for Educators: Online Social Networking Communities and Youth Risk." Center for Safe and Responsible Internet Use, 2006. http://www.cyberbully.org/cyberbully/docs/youthriskonlinealert.pdf/ (accessed December 15, 2009).

Wolak, Janis, Davis Finkelhor, and Kimberly Mitchell. "Trends in Arrests of Online Predators." Crimes Against Children Research Center (2009): 1–10, http://www.unh.edu/ccrc/pdf/CV194.pdf/ (accessed December 15, 2009).

WEBSITES

Center for Safe and Responsible Internet Use, http://www.cyberbully.org/

Common Sense Media, http://www.commonsensemedia.org/

Connect Safely, http://www.connectsafely.org/

Creative Commons, http://creativecommons.org/

Cyberbullying Research Center, http://www.cyberbullying.us/

CyberSmart, http://cybersmartcurriculum.org/

Digital Citizenship, http://www.digitalcitizenship.net/

Digizen, http://www.digizen.org/

Electronic Privacy Information Center, http://epic.org/privacy/bill_track.html/

GetNetWise, http://www.getnetwise.org/

GNU General Public License, http://www.gnu.org/licenses/gpl.html/

IKeepSafe, http://www.ikeepsafe.org/

iSafe, http://www.isafe.org/

National Crime Prevention Council, http://www.ncpc.org/cyberbullying/

NetSmartz, http://www.netsmartz.org/

STOP cyberbullying, http://stopcyberbullying.org/

A Thin Line, http://www.athinline.org/

WebWiseKids, http://www.webwisekids.org/

Wired Safety, http://www.wiredsafety.org/

8

◆ ◆ ◆

USING SOCIAL NETWORKING SITES TO CONNECT TEENS WITH YOUNG ADULT LITERATURE

Janet Hilbun

Youth services librarians often function as intermediaries between teens and literature. Many bemoan the fact that teens "just don't read anymore." Research, though, has proven this assumption false—teens do read. They may not be reading books, but they are reading (e.g., Braun 2007; Hughes-Hassell 2010).

Research shows that teens read constantly—text messages, e-mail, MySpace and Facebook, magazines, instant messages, and websites—as well as required school reading and books. Even teens who say they are non-readers or do not like to read spend a great part of each day actually reading (Braun 2007). The task of the librarian thus becomes one of finding ways of connecting young adult (YA) literature with the technology that teens immerse themselves in during their daily lives.

Libraries and librarians have met this challenge in a number of ways: library web pages; video book reviews or book trailers; online book clubs or literature circles; Second Life and other 3D social worlds; blogs; book sharing sites such as Shelfari, Goodreads, or LibraryThing; RSS feeds and twittering; and, of course, social networking sites such as Facebook and MySpace. Each of these tools can be used to connect teens to YA literature. Drawing a line, though, between types of social networking tools becomes difficult, as most creators of web pages, blogs, and pages on Facebook or MySpace link to other types of networking platforms as well.

LIBRARY WEB PAGES AS SOCIAL NETWORKING

With more and more young adults using the Internet rather than the library for research—both for school projects and personal information (Abbas et al. 2007), it becomes obvious that "if librarians want to attract young adults to their collections and services, they must become integral members of the online community. Furthermore, library web pages must address the needs of young adults on many levels—academic, social, and recreational" (Hughes-Hassell and Miller 2003, 145).

While developing a set of library web pages is relatively simple, it takes time to launch a site and even more time to keep it updated and to maintain it. Though some libraries use their teen advisory boards to help with this maintenance, more often the youth services librarian has responsibility for the site (Hughes-Hassell and Miller 2003). Many library administrators worry about teens adding unapproved or inappropriate content or accessing confidential library information, such as circulation records (Hughes-Hassell and Miller 2003).

Many library websites serve mainly informational purposes—promoting books and reading, providing homework help and reference services, announcing library events, giving links to community resources and access to recreational activities such as games, music, and e-zines. However, a large number of library websites also provide space for teens to publish reviews or creative writing and to interact with other teens (Hughes-Hassell and Miller 2003). The library website then goes from being merely an informational tool to a platform for promoting social networking among teens.

Designing Teen Library Web Pages That Promote Social Networking

Designing teen-friendly websites that use social networking tools to connect teens with YA literature involves more than just deciding what information to make available and more than just providing ways for teens to publish and interact with each other. Teen users are discriminating and expect ease of use as well as useful information and attractive design. If at all possible, teens should be involved with designing the website and choosing its content. According to Gorman and colleagues, the following elements should be considered in designing youth web pages:

- Do not overload your page with graphics and image maps that do not contribute in some way to the information on the page.
- Organize the material on your page into logical, clearly marked sections.
- Annotate all the sites you include on the page, describing what the patron will find if he or she clicks the given link. Make sure the URL is posted so that the page can be printed for further reference.
- Link to your library's subscription databases and provide extensive annotations of each source.
- Include local resources that a teen might not find anywhere else.
- Include information about upcoming programming or how teens can become involved with volunteering or on a teen advisory board.
- Create a place for teens to submit their own writing, including reviews of books, websites, video and computer games (Gorman, Suellentrop, and Jones 2004, 279).

What to Include on Teen Library Web Pages to Promote Reading

Most library teen websites include reviews of books, book trailers, lists of new books, and links to different award winner lists. Some websites include an instant messaging feature with the teen services librarian staying logged on during work hours. Other websites link to blogs or a teen space on Facebook or MySpace where teens can discuss what they are reading, thus creating an additional level of social networking and further connecting teens to literature.

For example, the Allen County Public Library in Fort Wayne, Indiana, has a teen page that includes many ways of connecting teens with literature. Pictures of new book titles link to the catalog and are further linked to LibraryThing for reviews and tagging. Patrons have a link enabling them to make their own comments and post reviews. The library also sponsors a Facebook page where teen patrons can post comments about books, movies, and library contests such as a book trailer contest sponsored by the library. The teen interface is almost a cross between a blog and a typical web page. Links to other blogs are included as well.

In Berkeley, California, the Berkeley Public Library web page also provides many avenues for teens to connect with YA literature. It includes a well-developed blog with several discussion threads, including a place for teens to post reviews and comment on books. "Tags" provide links to different book reviews and discussion threads. The teen home page of the Columbus Public Library in Columbus, Ohio, is wonderfully graphic and well thought out, with links to homework help, a blog, games, fun things to do, book reviews and book trailers. Teens must register for the interactive portions of the blog, the Express It page, and sign an agreement to abide by the site use guidelines. Librarians are also available for live chats.

Many other libraries have well-developed teen pages that serve as gateways to connecting teens with literature, libraries, and each other. Despite this, based on a recent search and review of U.S. public library teen web pages (see Jones and Pfeil 2004 for a selected list of web pages), there seem to be two common problems with many of these pages. The first is that many of them have not been updated in days, weeks, or months. Obviously this is a large deterrent to teen usage of these pages. The second is that even for the wonderfully designed pages that were well thought out and up to date at the time of the review, only a few teens were participating in the social networking venues. This problem is much more difficult to overcome and highlights a crucial issue: without active teen participation, libraries can have little success in using social networking tools to connect teens to YA literature.

BLOGS

Over the past couple of years, web logs, or blogs, have gained in ease of creation and in the number available on the Internet. The entries are usually brief and arranged chronologically on the page. Most blogs provide a way for readers to comment on the postings. This may involve registering or signing up in order to get a password to post comments. On the other hand, some blogs do not require setting up passwords for participation.

A majority of Internet users read at least one blog regularly, and many are bloggers themselves. According to Singer (2009) of *The Future Buzz*, 60% of people aged 18 to 44 blog, and there are over 200 million blogs available online. Because of the technological savvy of most teens, blogs can be an informal way of reaching teens and connecting them to books. According to Braun (2007, 38):

Teens read blogs to keep up with topics of interest, including technology, world news, and gossip. They read blogs written by friends and favorite authors. This reading is a way to collect information, find out about the world, and learn how people think and live.

For many, reading blogs is very similar to reading magazines as far as the types of information they are interested in learning.

More and more library teen pages include blogs. Blogs for Teens, for example, offers an extensive list of such blogs. Any library hosting a blog for teens can post the link there. Most of these library blogs include book reviews and other content to connect teens with books. But librarians are not the only people blogging for teens. Many adults blog about YA literature, as do teens themselves. Instead of or in addition to creating their own YA book blogs, libraries can link their websites to some of these preexisting resources.

Examples of Blogs That Promote Young Adult Literature

One very attractive and active book blog created by teens is 3 Evil Cousins: Book Reviews 4 and by Teens. This blog includes the following mission statement:

> Our Mission...or whatever. Hello and welcome to 3 Evil Cousins, where we plan to bring you reviews, interviews, and the occasional essay written *by* teens and *for* teens. Try out our new chat feature, let us know what you're reading or what books you can't wait for, and get in on our evil plot to make YA into the biggest section of the bookstore. Truly, yours! The Evil Ones.

An outstanding teen blog site dedicated to having teens read and write reviews is Flamingnet Book Reviews. It was begun by Seth Cassal in 2002, when he was a fifth grader and his father posted his reviews for him. Publishers began sending Seth books to review, and he enlisted other students to review with him. Now his reviewers come from 44 states in the United States and from various locations in England and Australia. Readers can post comments to any review or join community discussions on selected books. This blog also has a Facebook community.

A teen blog with a slightly different take is Steph Bowe's Hey! Teenager of the Year. Steph is a soon-to-be published teenager who has her own blog, website, and YouTube "station." She twitters and links to her reviews on Goodreads. Her blog mostly deals with encouraging teens to write and publish.

Among exemplary blogs created by adults to encourage teens to discuss teen literature there is Jennifer Hubert's Reading Rants: Out of the Ordinary Teen Booklists, which has been a Web presence since 1998. In 2008, it was made interactive with teens commenting on the reviewed books. The blog includes sections with links to other blogs called Book Review Websites and Blogs for Teens as well as links to Kids and Teen Lit Blogs for Grownups.

There is also Teen Ink, which is sponsored by the Young Authors Foundation. It has a blog to accompany its print publication. The blog invites students to participate, register, and submit work, both online and in print. It also provides links to its Facebook, Twitter, and MySpace pages.

YA authors themselves have also discovered that blogs provide a way to reach teens. Many YA author blogs or websites simply contain contact information so that readers can send letters. However, a number of them are interactive, with multiple ways for readers to connect with the authors. For example, popular YA author John Green and his brother have a blog that goes way beyond promoting reading. The Nerdfighter's website/blog/Ning network requires membership, and as of February of 2011 it had over 54,000 members. With interactive discussions, places to post pictures and videos, as well as John Green's blog, the website has what it takes to attract teens.

Laurie Halse Anderson's blog is more traditional. It shares her blog posts and enables teens to comment on them.

Libba Bray's blog uses an easy conversational style. It really shows her personality, such as the repeated image of a red Converse tennis shoe, and it contains links to YouTube videos and to her Twitter page. As with most author blogs, it allows comments from fans, and most of her postings receive many comments.

Scott Westerfeld is another author who has gone out of his way to make his blog really connect to YA readers. Besides having a forum for discussions, he has also instituted live meet-up sessions where readers can join him for chats. He also has links to his Facebook and Twitter pages.

Why Blogs Rule When It Comes to Promoting Young Adult Literature

Blogs "rule" as far as connecting teens to literature because most allow them to participate in the reading, reviewing, and commenting process. Attractive blog design—as well as the popularity of the author and/or the topic—tends to be key to connecting with teens. Providing links to excellent YA literature blogs benefits both teens and the library, as blogs promote literacy and writing skills while also promoting library resources.

VIDEO BOOK REVIEWS AND BOOK TRAILERS

Members of the YouTube generation (today's teens) are not only consumers of online videos but creators as well. According to a Pew Internet & Family Life Study, 57% of teens watch online videos (Lenhart 2006). Hundreds of millions of people both watch and post videos on YouTube and other video posting sites such as TeacherTube. Video book trailers posted on these sites, as well as on library websites, blogs, author pages, and publisher websites, are numerous. Many are professionally designed and are works of art, but many others have been created by teens for school assignments, contests, or just the love of a book.

Publisher-designed book trailers provide professionally produced book introductions. Usually narrated by the author of the featured selection, the artwork and quality are superb and can be found with a YouTube search by book title. The publisher websites do provide links to some of the videos, but generally these trailers are easier to find through YouTube searches. Some publishers, such as Simon & Schuster, have their own YouTube pages. Libraries can link their websites to these videos to promote featured and popular YA titles.

Typing in a book title on sites such as YouTube and TeacherTube yields a much broader range of trailers and reviews, most produced by readers. While many are school assignments, many more show a teenager's love for a book. Other sites, such as Bookscreen and Booktrailers, also provide venues for book trailers, although these often link to YouTube videos. Mark Geary of Dakota State University has a web page called Movies for Literacy. It has a large number of book trailers produced by students and featuring a range of YA titles, especially classics and required school reading. Schooltube is also a venue for the safe posting of book trailers, although this site is rather cumbersome to wade through. Trailer Spy, a relative newcomer to the book trailer websites, offers a wide variety of trailers and commentary for YA novels.

Librarians can foster teen participation in the creation of book trailers by providing a place to post videos and sponsoring contests with prizes and screenings. The King County Public Library System in King County,

Washington, sponsored their Read, Flip, Win contest to support their summer reading program and supplement their Read Three, Get One program, for which teens receive a free book for every three they review (Wooten 2009). Rather than having teens or staff create their own trailers, other libraries embed YouTube videos in their websites or provide links to YouTube or other video site book trailers.

ONLINE BOOK CLUBS AND LITERATURE CIRCLES

A book club or reading group is a collection of readers who participate in a regular discussion of books, usually an assigned title. Traditionally these clubs meet in the same room, and the club has a small number of members. While book clubs, in many different forms, have been around for many years, moving book clubs to digital interfaces helps to meet teens where they are. Online book clubs work similarly to online distance education classes. Members must enroll, and they read the same book. The moderator posts questions and discussion starters, and club members join for asynchronous discussion or for live chats.

Online book clubs have several advantages over the traditional form, especially when the club has an asynchronous component and readers do not have to meet at a certain time. Online book clubs provide readers more of a chance to find a group tailored to special reading interests or genres, as membership is not limited by physical location. On the other hand, the intimacy of face-to-face social interaction is missing.

Technologies That Support Online Book Clubs

Various platforms exist for mounting online book clubs. Discussions may take place via websites, blogs, interfaces such as Yahoo! or Google groups, or email listservs. Generally these groups are open to the public, and anyone can join.

Libraries, though, tend to prefer "safer" online environments. Moodle is a popular, free, open-source software used to manage book clubs and discussion groups. Moodle's website describes this software as

an Open Source Course Management System (CMS), also known as a Learning Management System (LMS) or a Virtual Learning Environment (VLE). [Moodle] has become very popular among educators around the world as a tool for creating online dynamic websites for their students. To work, it needs to be installed on a web server somewhere, either on one of your own computers or one at a web hosting company.

Since only registered users can access a Moodle-based book club environment, the book club leader can monitor membership and participation. The software allows for asynchronous discussions, synchronous or real-time chats, and profile spaces, and it can be easily accessed from computers with Internet connections (Scharber 2009). Unlike book clubs that are more open in the amount of time in which discussion occurs, libraries using Moodle tend to limit the club to a certain period of time and a specific book.

Online book clubs do take time to manage, especially if using an open web-based forum rather than a closed forum with limited access. Not only do you need time to set up the interface, choose the books, and find participants but book club discussions also require frequent monitoring. The book club's site must to be kept up to date and current. As a monitor or leader, you must be responsive and post frequently. Fostering additional ways for interaction also helps. Be sure to allow places for participants to post reviews or suggest books for further discussion, and have quizzes or discussion questions. Also make sure that the interface is attractively designed.

Many public libraries, such as the Pierce County Library System in Tacoma, Washington, the Camden County Library System, in Camden County, New Jersey, and Wisconsin's Waukesha County Federated Library System offer an interesting adaptation of library book clubs. These libraries use the DearReader subscription service as their book club interface. Starting each Monday, DearReader's staff e-mails a 5-minute segment of a book every day to participants so that, by the end of the week, two or three chapters have been distributed. All of the participating libraries receive the same books. Book group moderators invite guest hosts to share favorite books, but the forum does not allow for much discussion.

California's San Jose Public Library uses LibraryThing as the interface for their teen library club. Teens join LibraryThing, posts their books, and then join a discussion group forum that is open to any teen. Asynchronous in nature, it allows for the simultaneous discussion of several books.

Literature Circles

Literature circles, while similar to book clubs or book discussion groups, tend to be part of an academic or classroom environment and are usually more structured and formal. According to Hill and colleagues (2004),

> In literature circles, small groups of students gather together to discuss a piece of literature in depth. The discussion is guided by students' response to what they have read. ... Literature circles provide a way for students to engage in critical thinking and reflection.... Students reshape and add onto their understanding as they construct meaning with other readers.

Many teachers and school districts are experimenting with online environments for literature circles. In Texas, the San Antonio Independent School District has a well-structured program of online literature circles with classes from across the United States joining and pairing up with similar classes. It uses Moodle to host the circles because of child safety concerns. While literature circles tend to be done through the classroom, they might be a way for public libraries to connect with teachers and students for a joint venture.

BOOK-SHARING SOCIAL NETWORKS

Book-sharing social networks are a relatively new addition to the Internet. LibraryThing began in 2005, and Shelfari and Goodreads launched in late 2006. Sites such as Shelfari, LibraryThing, and Goodreads combine several social networking technologies. Besides creating a showcase for books, they allow for tagging, sharing, forming or joining groups, reviewing, and rating books. Many libraries use these types of social networking sites as a restricted platform for their book clubs, but there are also groups that anyone can join. Membership is free, and all three of these networks are easy to join.

While the three sites are similar, there are some differences. Goodreads purports to be the largest of the three with "more than 4,300,000 members who have added more than 120,000,000 books to their shelves." It is relatively easy to navigate, and it offers authors a space to join and promote their books in the form of a Goodreads web page and blog where readers can post comments. Neil Gaiman, Sara Dessen, Laurie Halse Anderson, and Tamora Pierce are some of the most popular teen authors on Goodreads. The site provides several options for sorting author pages: by popularity, by books authored, by last name, by last posted online, or by books on your personal shelf. Libraries or individuals can download a widget to link Goodreads to their library for ease in using this as a book club site. Goodreads also does the best job of organizing groups by category to make it easier to view how other libraries have set up their groups. Groups can be either public or private.

Shelfari is similar to Goodreads in that it allows you to "shelve" and share your books. Forming new discussion groups is easy, but to join private groups, readers have to be invited. A librarian could easily handle this by having a signup on the library web page and then inviting interested participants. While authors do not have web pages on Shelfari, author profiles can be posted and edited in a wiki-style platform. Shelfari also has a blog to promote new books and good reading.

LibraryThing rivals Goodreads in size. It allows you to catalog up to 200 books for free, but it charges for any additional books. Unlike Goodreads and Shelfari, it has a Zeitgeist overview page with numerous interesting statistics about LibraryThing: largest libraries, most reviewed books, authors on LibraryThing, most popular tags, number of users, number of books reviewed, and so on. Readers can join the author pages, which will link them to profiles of fans. An author page provides links to the authors' other websites and Twitter pages. The San Jose Public Library uses LibraryThing as the platform for its teen book club.

Libraries can use these book-sharing social network platforms in two ways. They can set up their own book clubs and link members to them through their library web pages, or they can recommend existing groups for their teens to join. While all three sites have ways to search for groups, all are rather cumbersome to use, and users must join them to sign up for a group.

Another use for these platforms would be to have teens use them to post their own reviews and bookshelves and to invite each other to be friends and share books. This way is less formal and can be time-consuming. On the other hand, it can be done without having a librarian run the group.

FACEBOOK, MYSPACE, AND NINGS

The use of social networking sites such as Facebook and MySpace has grown phenomenally in the last few years. Not only individuals join and create personal home pages but libraries and other groups also construct their own pages. As of early 2010, Facebook and MySpace still ranked as the top social networking sites (Brooks 2010), but there are actually hundreds of online social networks. Since Facebook and MySpace are the most popular, and because teens are so involved with them, libraries and librarians, authors, and publishers often find that they are tailor-made for reaching out to teens.

More so than the other social networking technologies discussed in this chapter, sites such as MySpace and Facebook offer versatility, but they also raise more concerns. For one thing, both of these venues have a minimum age of 13 in order to join and post a profile. Since the actual age of account holders cannot be monitored, many participants lie about their age if they do not meet the minimum age requirement (Gross 2009). The challenge thus becomes how to use these popular social networking technologies without encouraging young adults to lie.

The versatility of these sites—and the fact that there is no charge for using them—makes them popular for connecting teens to literature. This can be accomplished in several ways. Many libraries have Facebook and MySpace pages to announce events, post titles of new book arrivals, and share book reviews. People can sign up as fans, often without joining the networks. A great number of popular teen authors have a presence on both MySpace and Facebook. Readers can join as fans, but to receive status reports and posts or to take part in discussion groups, users must be members of the sites. Readers can also search the sites by book titles and find discussion forums for specific titles as well as links to authors' pages. Popular books such as Suzanne Collins's *Catching Fire* and Stephenie Meyer's *Twilight* have multiple discussions groups available. Both Facebook and MySpace enable any members to form groups. These groups can be made public or private, so a library can set up a discussion group just for invited members. A blog feature also adds ways for individuals or groups to have discussions.

As far as features available on the two sites, there is not a great deal of difference. MySpace has more blatant advertising and a more cluttered look than Facebook. MySpace also posts pictures on its home page, many of which are overtly provocative and which may be off-putting to some parents who monitor their teens' online activities. Facebook has a cleaner, simpler look, although it also has ads. MySpace allows for personalizing your homepage, while Facebook has a generic format. Neither one is particularly easy to navigate when one is looking to see if a group that could meet one's needs is already organized. If you know the exact title of an author or group, it is much easier to locate a particular person or web page. Librarians should explore the features of both sites before deciding which best fits their needs. They should also ask their teen patrons which platform they would prefer to use or already use.

Ning is an online platform for people to create their own social networks; it competes with MySpace and Facebook for users who want to create their own special interest groups. Use of the site can be free or fee-based depending on whether the group wants to allow or control the advertisements that are part of the free group hosting. YA author John Green's Nerdfighters is one of the largest groups on Ning.

While Nings may be visually rather busy, group moderators or creators can control membership in Ning groups and can activate optional features, such as ways to invite new members, an activity feed, RSS feeds, photos and videos, a chat feature, and discussion forum, as well as blogs for every member. The main issue with Ning is that searching for groups with unknown names is difficult, as there is no complete listing of the groups provided.

As with other social networking applications, the main issues with Facebook, MySpace, and Ning use are staff time and attracting members. To be useful, a page must be updated regularly. Reaching YA readers can also be an issue. The library must make sure not only that the group or page is easy to access but also that teens know that it is available. Good PR becomes an important factor. Networking with school librarians, writing newsletter entries, posting announcements and links on the main library web page, advertising in local or school newspapers, and providing library signage in the areas where teens congregate can help spread the word.

TWITTER AND RSS

Twitter is a microblogging service that allows people to stay connected via short messages delivered in multiple ways: cell phones, the Web, and instant messages. Posts are limited to 140 characters. According to the Twitter website, the purpose of Twitter messages is to answer the question "What's happening?" Members can choose whose messages they will receive and select which Twitter members can follow them online.

Twitter also has a blog to keep users updated about what the site team considers important, and it is not necessary to sign up for Twitter to access the blog. The site links to Google Blogger for those who want to create their own blogs. Widgets, buttons, and applications are available for mobile phones and websites.

Many YA authors twitter, and fans can sign up for the service and receive updates from favorite authors. While the site provides a list of authors and publishers, a name search finds even more authors. Sarah Dessen, Libba Bray, Cory Doctorow, and John Green are among the authors who twitter. Libraries could easily use Twitter to send information about programming and new books to teens. A link from the library web page enables teens to sign up easily to use this service.

The main drawback, though, is that Twitter seems to be more popular with adults than with teens. Teen usage has grown since the site began; but according to the *New York Times*, only about 11% of Twitter users are aged 12 to 18 (Miller 2009), and many more teens text than twitter.

Similarly, RSS feeds (Really Simple Syndication) provide a method to publish updated blog entries, headlines, videos, and so on in an easily accessible format. These feeds allow readers to subscribe to updates from popular websites and blogs. The user must download a "feeder" or "aggregator" and then subscribe to a feed. This feeder checks the user's feeds regularly for new entries and downloads the entries by sending them to the user's e-mail. For the web page creator, enabling an RSS feed is also simple.

Libraries can use RSS feeds to send subscribers updates on programming, new acquisitions, or reviews. As with most of the technology discussed in this chapter, the information is easy to disseminate, but it is much more difficult to attract users.

AVATARS, SECOND LIFE, AND OTHER MUVEs

Second Life is a multiuser virtual environment, or MUVE. While this technology has been around since 2003, few libraries have adopted it as a form of building community or promoting reading. One exception is the Public Library of Charlotte- Mecklenburg, North Carolina, which operated an island on Teen Second Life from 2006 to 2009 designed to "build community" in a technical environment and explore library services in a 3D space (Czarnecki 2008). However, the project ended in 2009 owing to low patron participation (see chapter 11 for details).

While there are other less well known MUVEs, Second Life has the advantage of having a separate space for teens aged 13 to 17. All adults in Teen Second Life must pass a background check before being allowed on the "island" and cannot visit other islands on the teen grid (Czarnecki 2008). Once a person joins, he or she creates an avatar, who then "lives" in the Second Life environment. While they are in regular Second Life universes, residents develop a persona, spend money for goods, land, and services, and create a new life. The Charlotte Mecklenburg Library used Second Life not only for role playing but also as a programming venue and for soliciting teen input on programming. Ideas for use included bringing in teen authors to make presentations via Second Life and staffing a virtual reference desk (Czarnecki 2008).

Library uses for this technology are still in their infancy. Librarians who have the money to purchase an island or who can partner with an agency that will fund it have the opportunity to provide creative programming that can further connect teens to libraries and literature.

CONCLUSION: WHERE DO WE GO FROM HERE?

Web 2.0 and social networking technologies definitely have a place in connecting teens to literature, but we may ask "If we build it, will they come?" The answer is a resounding Maybe. Most of today's teens are technologically savvy and use these technologies in a variety of ways. Websites, blogs, YouTube, and social networking sites such as MySpace and Facebook do support connecting teens to authors and literature, but they must be promoted, not just made available. While these are useful tools for librarians, they may not be successful in engaging teens without the personal connection of the library and the librarian to the teen patrons. As a result, getting input from teens is essential to making successful use of these technologies in promoting YA literature.

The YA librarian must be a visible part of the use of these technologies so that the teens still feel that personal connection. Good design and frequent site updates are almost mandatory. It is also necessary to meet the teens where they are—whether it is on a blog, a website, an online book group, YouTube, Facebook, or Twitter. Find out the technologies your teens use most frequently and use these as a guide to where and how you decide to promote reading and literature.

Also remember that gimmicks work. Teens like contests and winning prizes. Competitions for the best book trailer or blog entry are relatively easy to institute. Invite an author to join an online book group or book blog group for a chat. Many authors will do this for free, as it does not involve travel. Have a book of the month promoted with a simple quiz that readers can take online; the winner of the random drawing from quiz takers gets a copy of the book.

Using social networks to promote books and reading to teens takes time and commitment as well as planning, but it can—and does—work. Most social networking technologies are free or inexpensive. Add teens and their ideas, good books, interesting authors, and a creative librarian, and you have a recipe for success.

REFERENCES

Abbas, J., M. Kimball, G. D'Elia, and K. G. Bishop. "Public Libraries, the Internet and Youth: Part 1. Internet Access and Youths' Use of the Public Library." *Public Libraries* 46, no. 4 (July/August 2007): 40–45.

Braun, Linda. "Hotspot: LOL@yourlibrary." *Young Adult Library Services* 5, no. 4 (Summer 2007): 38–40.

Brooks, Mark. Social Networking Watch, http://www.socialnetworkingwatch.com/usa-social-networking-ran.html/ (accessed February 20, 2010).

Czarnecki, Kelly. "Building Community as a Library in a 3D Environment." *Australasian Public Library and Information Services* 21, no. 1 (March 2008): 25–27.

Gorman, Michelle, Tricia Suellentrop, and Patrick Jones. *Connecting Young Adults and Libraries*, 3rd ed. New York: Neal Schuman, 2004.

Gross, Doug. "Social Networks and Kids: How Young is too Young?" In CNN [database online], 2009, http://cnn.com/2009/TECH/11/02/kids.social.networks/index.html/ (accessed January 22, 2010).

Hill, Bonnie Campbell, Katherine L. Schlick Noe, and Nancy J. Johnson. "Overview of Literature Circles," 2004, http://www.litcircles.org/Overview/overview.html/ (accessed January 21, 2010).

Hughes-Hassell, Sandra. "Developing a Leisure Reading Program That Is Relevant and Responsive to the Lives of Urban Teenagers: Insights from Research." In *Urban Teens in the Library*, edited by Denise E. Agosto and Sandra Hughes-Hassell, 41–52. Chicago: American Library Association, 2010.

Hughes-Hassell, Sandra, and Ericka Thickman Miller. "Public Library Websites for Young Adults: Meeting the Needs of Today's Teens Online." *Library & Information Science Research* 25, no. 2 (Summer 2003): 143–56.

Jones, Patrick, and Angela Pfeil. "Public Library YA Webpages for the Twenty-First Century." *Young Adult Library Services* 2, no. 2 (Spring 2004): 14–18.

Lenhart, Amanda. "User-Generated Content." Washington, DC: Pew Research Center's Internet & American Life Project, http://www.pewinternet.org/Presentations/2006/UserGenerated-Content.aspx# (accessed February 23, 2009).

Miller, Claire Cain. "Who's Driving Twitter's Popularity? Not Teens." *The New York Times*, August 26, 2009.

Scharber, Cassandra. "Online Book Clubs: Bridges Between Old and New Literacies' Practices." *Journal of Adolescent and Adult Literacy* 52, no. 5 (February 2009): 433–37.

Singer, Adam. "70 Usable Stats from the 2009 State of the Blogosphere." *The Future Buzz*, http://thefuturebuzz.com/2009/12/10/blogging-stats-facts-data/ (accessed January 9, 2010).

Wooten, Jennifer. "Flipped! Want to get Teens Excited about Summer Reading? Just Add Video." *School Library Journal* 55, no. 5 (May 2009): 38–40.

WEBSITES

Allen County Public Library teen page, http://acplteens.wordpress.com/
Berkeley Public Library, http://www.berkeleypubliclibrary.org/content/
Blogs for Teens, http://www.libsuccess.org/index.php?title=Blogs_for_Teens/
Bookscreen, http://bookscreening.com/
Booktrailers, http://booktrailers.blogspot.com/
Camden County Library System, http://www.camden.lib.nj.us/readers/online
      bookclub.htm/
Columbus Public Library, http://teens.columbuslibrary.org/
DearReader subscription service, http://www.dearreader.com/
Facebook, http://www.facebook.com/
Flamingnet Book Reviews, http://www.flamingnet.com/
The Future Buzz, http://thefuturebuzz.com/2009/12/10/blogging-stats-facts-data/
Goodreads, http://www.goodreads.com/about/us/
Hey! Teenager of the Year, http://heyteenager.blogspot.com/
Laurie Halse Anderson's blog, http://halseanderson.livejournal.com/
Libba Bray's blog, http://libba-bray.livejournal.com/
LibraryThing, http://www.LibraryThing.com/
LibraryThing overview page, http://www.librarything.com/zeitgeist/
LibraryThing discussion forum, http://www.LibraryThing.com/groups/luv2read/
Moodle, www.moodle.org/
Movies for Literacy, http://www.homepages.dsu.edu/mgeary/booktrailers/
      adolescent.htm/
MySpace, http://www.myspace.com/
Nerdfighters, http://nerdfighters.ning.com/
Ning, www.ning.com/
Pierce County Library System, http://www.supportlibrary.com/su/su.cfm?x=
      204304&g=/su/banners/Pierce_OBC.jpg&cb=8EB3DD&cs=003C7F&q/
Reading Rants, http://www.readingrants.org/
San Antonio Independent School District, http://itls.saisd.net/index.php?option=
      com_content&task=view&id=78&Itemid=101/
San Jose Public Library teen book club, http://www.sjlibrary.org/gateways/
      teens/bookclub.htm/
Scott Westerfeld's blog, http://scottwesterfeld.com/blog/
Second Life, http//www.secondlife.com/
Shelfari, www.shelfari.com/
Simon & Schuster, http://www.youtube.com/user/SimonSchusterVideos/
Teacher Tube, http://www.teachertube.com/
Teen Ink, http://www.teenink.com/
3 Evil Cousins: Book Reviews 4 and by Teens, http://www.3evilcousins.blogspot.
      com/
Trailer Spy, http://www.trailerspy.com/trailers/basic/mr/327/Young-Adult/
Twitter, http://twitter.com/
Waukesha County Federated Library System, http://www.wcfls.lib.wi.us/
      forstaff/bookclubs.htm/
YouTube, http://www.youtube.com/

9

⬦ ⬦ ⬦

FANDOM AS A FORM OF SOCIAL NETWORKING

Elizabeth Burns

Many young adult (YA) authors have social network pages where fans can read about their lives, their interests, and their newest books. This chapter shows librarians how to find these resources and offers suggestions for using them with teens to get teens excited about reading. Before we discuss the social networking sites that most authors and their publishers use, it is helpful to explain what fandom is and what fansites offer teen fans.

WHAT IS FANDOM?

There are those who may not have heard of fandom, but that doesn't mean that they have never encountered or even participated in fan activities. At different times in life, most people become fans of something. It can be a book, a movie, or a television show, or whatever else they enjoy. Maybe it's a must-see television show or a must-read book series. At some point, just sitting back and reading or watching isn't enough. The person wants something more. Maybe she is reading *Beautiful Creatures* (2009) by Kami Garcia and Margaret Stahl and starts making sketches of what she thinks the main character Ethan Wate looks like. Those inspired drawings are fan art.

Perhaps someone is reading *Hunger Games* (2008) by Suzanne Collins. It's not the main characters of Peeta and Katniss that have this reader thinking; it's the story of Katniss's younger sister Prim that the reader cannot get out of his mind. For example, Prim is left behind as Katniss battles to the death in Prim's place. The reader may wonder, "Does Prim feel guilty? Relieved? Angry?" Wondering leads to writing, and suddenly there is a story about Prim. That story is fan fiction, also called fanfiction or fanfic.

A further way that fans adapt fiction work for their own expressions is called cosplay, or costume play. It involves dressing in costume inspired by a character. For example, the world and drawings of *Leviathan* (2009) by Scott Westerfeld, illustrated by Keith Thompson, may lead the reader to thinking, "Wow! I love those steampunk clothes! I wonder if I can put together an outfit like the ones Deryn wears?"

As another example of how fans engage with fiction, there is the reader who is fascinated by the political interactions of the Wizard and Muggle Worlds of the *Harry Potter* books by J. K. Rowling. She reads and rereads those passages, analyzing the politics and trying to reconcile what is said in different books to get an idea of the education, health, and other government areas. Or there is the childhood reader of the *Betsy-Tacy-Tib* books by Mary Hart Lovelace (1940), who, as an adult, goes on a vacation to all the spots Betsy visited during her early-20th-century European tour.

Any of these examples in isolation is about fans embracing the art, the story they have been captivated with, and acting on it. It is something they are doing themselves. They are being fans, but they are alone in what they are doing.

What happens when there are two people engaging in these activities? Perhaps two friends begin swapping fan fiction stories back and forth, offering corrections such as "That's not so-and-so's last name" or "That birthday is wrong." Or, a lunchtime table of friends spend their lunch hour dissecting the Cullen family history, trying to put together a cohesive timeline of what happened to the Cullens before Bella moved to Forks in Stephenie Meyer's *Twilight* (2005). The "facts" that they are relying on, from source material such as books, is called the canon.

The person who shares or swaps fanfic is no longer alone. She is now part of a group, a community—a fandom. While fans and fannish behavior (writing stories, talking about favorite books, obsessing over some aspect of a creative work) have existed since, well, since there have been things for people to be enthusiastic about, the Internet has allowed people to connect and create in ways they have not be able to in the past, on websites, bulletin boards, blogs, and listservs. The two people swapping fan fiction stories are now doing so from across the country. They have never actually met in real life—that is, in person. The group of friends meeting at lunchtime have, instead, turned themselves into a chat room in today's online communication environment.

Something that had been internal (enthusiasm for a book) expressed externally (a story, a picture, a *Doctor Who* scarf) now includes an aspect of socialization that has a built-in social network of others who love what the fans do and who understand that passion. What's also great about this type of intense reading of books is that it's educational. Learning how to dig deep into a work of literature, to cite sources, and to analyze the text are all things that teens do in school for English classes. Fan passion increases their engagement in these activities and leads them to learn even more.

COMMUNITY IN FANDOM

Social networking is one of the reasons that a fan experience shifts from something personal to something involving community, the shift from simply being a casual fan to a member of fandom. Once that social interaction starts taking place, there are many opportunities for people to participate. Those opportunities can be created by fans, by libraries, and even by the authors and publishers of books.

For many, the first step toward fandom is fan fiction, writing something that is set in someone else's imagination, using a world and characters and plot created by another. Those unfamiliar with it may see it as a waste of time for both the writer and reader and wonder why the time isn't spent reading good books. But for those who read fan fiction and create it, the answer is simple. It's written because it's fun; it's written because it continues the relationship with a book even after the book has ended; it's written because it fills a need. Sometimes, it is a way for someone who wants to be a writer to master the craft by concentrating on one building block of a story at a time. Depending on what the writer writes, he or she can use preexisting characters, plots, and settings. Whether using existing characters with an original plot or using an existing plot and adding a new character, it's similar to learning how to juggle. The writer starts with one ball and slowly adds others.

This is all good, but what about it is social? What is social about reading and writing? Aren't they uniquely individual experiences?

The fan fiction writer gets an idea for a story, a "what if." Instead of simply thinking about it, the person writes it down. If the process ends there, it remains an individual fan experience and has nothing to do with fandom, as fandom is always a shared experience.

To use a personal example, when I was in middle school, I wondered "What if the people from *Battlestar Galactica* met the people from *Star Trek*?" and I wrote a chapter or two. This was back when only the original series existed, by the way. That epic tale, which was never finished, has been lost. It never went anywhere other than my three-subject notebook. One lonely author, no readers. It shows how much I enjoyed those two shows and gives me a little geek credit, but at no point did that make me a member of any fandom, as it lacked the community sharing aspect of fandom.

What happens when the writer discovers that he or she is not alone in thinking "what if"? That someone else is also interested in exploring those ideas, but instead of just writing the story, this person also wants to read other people's creations? In the days before the Internet when I wrote my short-lived fan fiction, there wasn't an easy way to find others who shared that obsession beyond those in my school or neighborhood. Today, with the Internet and countless active online fan communities, it is as easy as accessing the Internet to find others with shared interests.

Let's go back to that solitary event, writing fan fiction. The writer goes online and finds FanFiction.net, an archive of all types of fan fiction for everything from anime to books, television to games. As is explained in detail in FanFiction.net's terms of service, anyone can read the stories, and anyone over the age of 13 can register and upload a story. FanFiction.net offers great quantity because it accepts so many stories. Guidelines for content and terms of service offer new writers some guidance on what to do and what not to do. For example, FanFiction.net doesn't accept works with explicit content or stories based on the work of authors who have said that they do not want fan fiction based on their works to be archived. The negative part of the quantity of stories available at Fanfiction.net is that the minority of high-quality stories are not easy to find among the huge number of stories available. All proofreading and editing is left up to the author. Pacing may be uneven; words might be misspelled; grammar rules are sometimes ignored; and stories may be incomplete. The writer may be overjoyed to find a place where it is easy to publish a story and begin getting feedback, but the reader may be overwhelmed to find such an overload of stories.

In any case, the writer finds FanFiction.net and realizes—"I am not alone!" He or she then posts the story. This is the start of joining a group, of interaction, of commenting on, and getting commented on. It's possible because of the social networking aspect of the archive, which includes the ability to comment on stories. The good thing about sharing a story is that the author gets feedback. Likewise, the bad thing about sharing a story is that the author gets feedback. Critical feedback quickly turns educational, and it isn't long before the writer finds out about "beta readers," or editors. This is one more step into fandom, into community, because now a direct relationship is made between a writer and his or her beta. A beta reader will read a story prior to publication. She will proofread the fan fiction story, check spelling and grammar, point out problems with the plot or characterization, double-check the canon, and do other things to make the story better and stronger. Because different beta readers may have different interests and strengths, it is possible for one story to have multiple beta readers. Look at how the online community has grown beyond just the writer: a writer, readers, commentators, and a beta reader!

FANDOM AS COMMUNITY DISCUSSION

FanFiction.net is just one place to go to find this type of community. There are other general archives as well as archives and websites that are all about one specific book or movie. Fan fiction stories are not the only things people may share. Drawings of characters and settings can be uploaded onto websites, archived, and shared as well.

Fan fiction and fan art are two ways to participate in fandom. Another just as important way is through, well, talking about the story. Online social media tools are used to share information and news, to talk, and just to hang out and have fun on the Internet. Fans create websites, blogs, LiveJournals, and wikis; they use message boards, chat rooms, and Twitter. Fans talk about the books they love, going deeper than "I loved it" or "I hated it." They analyze the texts. The community and fandom inspire them to dig even deeper than they would have on their own—much like a good English teacher who makes a book discussed in class more meaningful than a book read alone.

For example, the Harry Potter Lexicon has an entire section devoted to essays, ranging from "comedy to literary analysis." The literary analysis ranges from a close look at family connections in "Arthur Weasley's Relationship to Sirius Black: First Forays into the Black Family Tree," by fan Sylvie Augustus, to an examination of "Merlin, God, and You-Know-Who: Religion in the Wizarding World," by fan glamourousgeek. As can be seen by the names, online fans often use pseudonyms.

FANDOM AND POPULAR BOOKS: *HARRY POTTER* AND *TWILIGHT*

Two of the biggest fandoms at present are built around two of the biggest fantasy series for teenagers: the *Harry Potter* series by J. K. Rowling and the *Twilight* books by Stephenie Meyer. Both fandoms began with the books in the series; the successful movies have made large fandoms even bigger. A recent Google search of "Harry Potter fansites" resulted in 503,000 results. Fans can and do create any type of site they want to, but many fans create targeted websites that reflect their individual interests. Fans may work together to run these websites.

For example, The Harry Potter Lexicon website is basically a reference source for anything mentioned in the *Harry Potter* books. It answers questions such as: What spells are mentioned, and in what books? What plants are mentioned? Who does Mr. Weasley work with, and in what books do these characters appear? Steve Vander Ark, founder of the site, explains that he began his fan work by cataloging the *Harry Potter* books in paper notebooks, and then created The Harry Potter Lexicon in 2000 to move the data online (Vander Ark and Hobbs 2009). Updating and maintaining the website is such a huge project that Vander Ark no longer runs it alone. The decision to turn the website into a book triggered a lawsuit that brought fandom, especially the *Harry Potter* fandom, to the attention of the mainstream media. The details of that lawsuit are discussed later in this chapter in the section "Fandom and Legal Issues."

Another Harry Potter fansite that covers just about everything is MuggleNet. Or, if your teen patrons are looking for fan fiction just about *Harry Potter,* suggest Fiction Alley. Do they want news about the books, J. K. Rowling, the movies, or the actors in the movies? Suggest that they read the Leaky Cauldron website.

Or maybe they are interested in *Twilight*? Just like with *Harry Potter,* there are fansites just for *Twilight* fan fiction, such as Twilighted. Do you have an adult patron who wants to talk to other adults about *Twilight*? Twilight Moms, despite its name, welcomes all adults, not just "Moms" and not just women. As with *Harry Potter,* there is a Twilight Lexicon, except instead of wizard spells it is full of vampire and werewolf mythology. Looking for news about the next movie? The *Twilight* lover can read either Touched by *Twilight* or *Twilight* Source.

OTHER BOOK FANDOMS OF PARTICULAR INTEREST TO TEENS

Any books that capture the imaginations of readers will have a fandom. Megan Whalen Turner is a highly regarded, award-winning fantasy author for children and teens. The first book in her "The Queen's Thief" series (more commonly known as the Attolia series), *The Thief* (1996), won a Newbery Honor. In 2010, the fourth book in this series, *A Conspiracy of Kings*, was published. Unlike the *Harry Potter* and *Twilight* series, the Attolia series has not been turned into a high-profile, successful movie. The long wait between new books and the lack of multimedia tie-ins are reflected in a smaller fandom. A Google search of Attolia fansites returned just 300 results. Reading through just the first handful of sites showed that they aren't all separate fansites, something which is also true about the *Harry Potter* and *Twilight* fansites. Instead, reviews and websites keep pointing toward one fansite, Eddis, Attolia, Sounis. It's only one website, but it is where all the dedicated, obsessed, caring fans go to share news, fanfiction, fanart, and to analyze the books.

Other books and series with fan websites include *The Vampire Diaries* by L. J. Smith, which started as a book series in the 1990s. With vampires becoming all the rage, it has inspired a new wave of readers as well as a television show and fan websites that include the fans of both books and the television show, such as Vampire Diaries.Net. The *Percy Jackson and the Olympians* series by Rick Riordan is a popular book series that was turned into a film. Both the Blue Trident fansite and Camp Halfblood, an online version of the camp Percy Jackson attends, are online sources of fan news and fan fun. Fans of the Redwall series by Brian Jacques can gather and contribute to the Redwall Wiki. The popular Warrior series by Erin Hunter has a fan-created encyclopedia.

Whether it's one website or a hundred or a thousand, and whatever the size of the fandom, the fans have one thing in common: intense passion.

FANS, AUTHORS, AND FANDOM

Fandom has traditionally been driven by fans. People wanting to discuss a book, wanting to create a story—all is driven because the readers fall for a book. Falling in love with a book enough to engage in fannish activities isn't like other reading experiences. It's not like loving a book, or thinking it's the year's best, or recommending it to friends. It's about something more; it's the difference between having friends and falling in love. An author may want people to read their books and buy them; an author may want fans; and an author may gain fans by writing an excellent book. But an excellent book is not necessarily one that will inspire fandom. The book must inspire passion.

For example, the Michael L. Printz Award for Excellence in Young Adult Literature is awarded annually by the Young Adult Library Services Association, a division of the American Library Association. The award is given to a book that "exemplifies literary excellence in young adult literature." The books that win this award are often loved and admired by readers, and are frequently added to summer reading lists and discussed in classrooms. However, none of the Printz winners have yet inspired the fan behavior of *Harry Potter* or *Twilight*.

More than any other genre, fantasy novels, especially multivolume titles, seem to generate this level of passion, leading readers to create fan websites. While there are fandoms for nonfantasy works, fantasy is the inspiration for most book fandoms. *Harry Potter*, *Twilight*, and *Attolia* are all fantasy series. Perhaps it is the detailed worlds that are created for a fan to play in, to wonder, for instance, "What is happening back home while Frodo goes on his adventure?" that draw them in. Perhaps it is the appeal of a unique world different from one's own that attracts them.

Fans drive the fandom. They are inspired, so they create the websites. Often they put together reference sites such as the Harry Potter Lexicon, complete with family trees and timelines not just for the main characters but also for supporting characters. Authors typically aren't involved in the creation of fansites. J. K. Rowling didn't ask for this to happen, but it did. The fandom is about the fan experience, not about the author.

Some fans even have a love/hate experience with the author, especially for a series in which the author writes something that fans don't like. Some fans were furious about Stephenie Meyer's fourth and final *Twilight* book, *Breaking Dawn* (2008). Many aspects of the plot and characterization, as well as the ultimate resolution of the book and series, displeased them. Fans were not just attached to the story; they wanted certain things to happen. When these desires were not met—and it would have been impossible for an author to meet all the varied, sometimes competing expectations—the fans were loud and vocal. As reported by MTV, "One fast reader expressed her disappointment in the book by launching a discussion on Amazon.com urging fellow disgruntled fans: 'Don't burn your copies of the book—RETURN THEM'" (Weiss and Gonzalez 2008).

Authors have various understandings and beliefs about fandom, especially fan fiction. If the first rule of fandom is often said to be: "Don't talk about fandom," the second is "Don't send what you do to the author."

Why is "don't talk about fandom" the first rule? In the 1999 film *Fight Club* (based on the 1996 novel of the same name by Chuck Palahniuk), the character Tyler Durden says "Welcome to Fight Club. The first rule of Fight Club is: you do not talk about Fight Club. The second rule of Fight Club is: you DO NOT talk about Fight Club!" Fandom participants are aware of the shadowy area they play in. Talking about fandom—especially publicly—invites attention. From someone outside of fandom, that attention is often negative. "Why are you doing that?" "Isn't that a waste of time?" people ask fandom participants, and for fan fiction writers, "Shouldn't you be writing something original?"

Copyright holders, especially authors, have varying levels of acceptance and tolerance of fan fiction. To talk about fan fiction could invite not only anger from an author, but also attempts to remove online fan fiction based on that author's work. Most fan fiction participants don't want to risk the ire of authors. They also don't want to risk losing the ability to easily share and read fan fiction online. As explained earlier, archive sites such as FanFiction.net pay attention to authors' requests not to archive writing and art based on their work.

As reported in an interview in the *Wall Street Journal*, Annie Proulx's reaction to discovering fan fiction based on *Brokeback Mountain* illustrates the negative reactions of some authors:

> There are countless people out there who think the story is open range to explore their fantasies and to correct what they see as an unbearably disappointing story. They constantly send ghastly manuscripts and pornish rewrites of the story to me, expecting me to reply with praise and applause for "fixing" the story. ... They do not understand the original story, they know nothing of copyright infringement—i.e., that the characters Jack Twist and Ennis Del Mar are my intellectual property. (Proulx, as quoted in Hughes 2008)

Other authors understand fan fiction and fan communities because of their own participation. Meg Cabot, author of books for children and young adults, encourages fans to write fan fiction based on her work, but discourages them from sending their work to her. She summed it up in a November 5, 2003, posting to her blog explaining that she wrote fan fiction based on *Star Wars* as a youth, so she understands the appeal of writing it:

> I must, however, decline your invitations to read it. Because for some reason, reading other people's stories about my characters makes me feel very sweaty and nauseous (possibly why George [Lucas] didn't use any of my ideas?). So carry on. Just don't count on my input. My nervous system thanks you.

OFFICIAL FANDOM RESOURCES

Fandom is driven by fans. An author cannot create a fandom, but some authors have realized that they can provide their fans with some of the "more" they are seeking. Stephenie Meyer provides a lot of that "more" on her official website. Here a *Twilight* lover can find photographs of the Cullen cars as well as the dresses the girls in the book wore to the prom. Meyer has a playlist of songs she listened to while writing the book, as she feels the music fits the book experience. Tracking down the cars mentioned in books, sketching dresses based on a description, matching songs to books— these are all things that fans traditionally think about, track down, and put together. Meyer's doing this doesn't take away from the reader's fandom experience. Instead, it feeds the fan's belief that the book experience is more than what is found between the covers of the book. It tells the fan, "I, the author, also think this is important. I also think about this." Meyer's putting together a playlist doesn't stop a fan from doing so; if anything, it gives fans yet another thing to talk about. Are the song choices right or wrong? What songs would be better? Is it a song or musician or band unfamiliar to the reader? If it is, that's a whole other area of discussion.

Kami Garcia and Margaret Stohl are the authors of *Beautiful Creatures* (2009), the first book in a fantasy series set in present-day South Carolina. The authors have their own websites, a website for the book, a Facebook page for the book, and a book Ning. The publisher also has an official website for *Beautiful Creatures*. There is also an official fansite called The Caster Girls (& Boys), because there are "casters" (people with supernatural powers) in the book.

These various online sites provide ready-made opportunities for fans to interact with each other and the authors through posts and chats. Instead of fans creating their own social networks using existing resources, it has already been done for them. Like Meyer, Garcia and Stohl and their publisher, Little Brown, provide information and reference material not found in the book. For example, the town of Gatlin, South Carolina, is an important part of the book, so the publishers have a map online at the publisher's website. The authors' website, meanwhile, has photographs for those who want to "see" the world of Gatlin and *Beautiful Creatures*. The book website by the authors has playlists listing the songs that the characters listen to in the book.

As with Meyer's fansites, nothing stops a fan from drawing their own, more detailed map, from creating their own drawings of what they think the houses, people, and places of Gatlin look like, or from putting together a playlist on their own. Nothing stops them from going to LiveJournal to create their own blogs or discussion forums, and nothing prevents them from creating their own websites. The authors and publishers understand and appreciate that fans are going to congregate online and form communities, so why not have established places for them to do so?

The creation and maintenance of these official online places often starts before a book is published. The official websites for *Beautiful Creatures* were established before the book's publication date of December 2009. *Beautiful Creatures* debuted at number three on the *New York Times* bestseller list. At this point, it is impossible to tell the impact of the authors' and publishers' sites on fans and any potential fandom for the book. What is apparent, however, is that authors and publishers are taking fandom seriously.

While officially most authors don't want to see fan fiction, every now and then an official fan fiction contest is part of the promotion for a book. For example, in 2005 the book distributor Baker & Taylor sponsored a fan fiction contest to promote Laurie Halse Anderson's book *Prom* (2005). Teens were asked to write a prequel, sequel, or alternate ending to *Prom*.

Book trailers—videos about books—are also being used to promote books. Just like a trailer for a movie entices viewers to see the movie, book trailers are produced to get people interested in reading a book, rather than recapping the entire book. Book trailers may be author made or publisher created. For example, Maggie Stiefvater produced her own book trailer for *Shiver*, which can be viewed at Stiefvater's website. Later, her publisher created an official book trailer, which is on the publisher's website. Shannon Hale ran a book trailer contest for *Rapunzel's Revenge*, asking for book trailers and then letting people vote for their favorites at her website.

Other examples of publisher-created tie-in content include Scholastic's website for *The Hunger Games* (2008) by Suzanne Collins. In *The Hunger Games*, teenagers enter a contest and battle for survival. Only one contestant will walk away alive. So what does Scholastic have on its website?

A virtual *Hunger Games*. When the player makes a wrong choice—and most of the choices are wrong choices—he or she is told, "You weren't ready for the *Hunger Games*." Book-related items are also available for download on the website, including icons and wallpapers. Icons and wallpapers are among the type of art that inspired fans create, so here is another example of a publisher providing fan items to the fans.

FANDOM AND LEGAL ISSUES

Because people cannot legally publish their fan fiction and make money from it, many think that creating anything fan-related is illegal, shouldn't be done, and certainly shouldn't be encouraged. This chapter cannot give legal advice, but there are some legal points to keep in mind when promoting online fandom for teen library users.

Copyright law offers authors copyright protection over their works. As explained on the website for the U.S. Copyright Office, copyright protects original works of authorship. As long as a book is under copyright, who makes money on the work is defined by the terms of the contract. (Typically the publisher and/or the author have this right, depending on the particular contract.) This protection extends to derivative works. In other words, only J. K. Rowling can publish a book about Harry Potter; only Stephenie Meyer can publish a book about Edward Cullen; and only Kami Garcia and Margaret Stohl can publish a sequel to *Beautiful Creatures*.

There are exceptions to copyright. Notably there is "fair use," which indicates that small portions of works can be used, such as quotes, for commentary, criticism, news reporting, and scholarly writing. Published essays and articles about original works often fall under fair use.

What is and is not fair use was litigated in 2007 and 2008 in the Harry Potter Lexicon lawsuit. J. K. Rowling (as the owner of the copyright for the *Harry Potter* books) and Warner Bros. (as the filmmakers and owners of the images in the *Harry Potter* movies) sued RDR Books, the publisher for the book version of Steve Vander Ark's online The Harry Potter Lexicon. The plaintiffs argued that the proposed book was both a violation of copyright and a violation of fair use. Much was made of how much of the language from the *Harry Potter* books appeared, unchanged, in the proposed Lexicon book, as well as how much (or how little) analysis was included (Eligon 2008).

A trial judge determined that a reference book such as the proposed Lexicon book was acceptable as a "transformative" work, but that this particular book did not fall under "fair use" because of the amount of verbatim copying from the source material. Steve Vander Ark revised the manuscript accordingly and published the revised content as a book in 2009. (The legal documents in the case are available at the Houghton Mifflin website).

Another exception to copyright protection that allows a noncopyright holder to publish a work is when the work is a parody or satire. In 2001, Houghton Mifflin sought to publish *The Wind Done Gone* (2001) by Alice Randall. Randall told the story of *Gone with the Wind* (1936) from the point of view of a slave on Scarlett O'Hara's plantation. The copyright holders of *Gone with the Wind* sued to stop publication of the book, arguing it was an unauthorized sequel. Houghton Mifflin argued that the work was a parody. Houghton Mifflin has archived information about the legal dispute at its website. The publisher claimed that Randall's book was a parody, not a sequel:

> Randall wrote her book to comment critically on a novel that she feels has harmed generations of African Americans. ... *The Wind Done Gone* is an ingeniously executed parody that, in telling its own story, turns *Gone With the Wind* upside down and inside out and explodes that work's familiar stereotypes along the way. *The Wind Done Gone* does not, as any sequel would, exploit the reader's love of the original work; instead it makes readers question the reasons for that love, if it ever existed.

An injunction was granted against publication, but the Court of Appeals overturned it. The parties ultimately settled out of court. *The Wind Done Gone* was published, bearing the subtitle *An Unauthorized Parody*.

There are also instances in which a work is based on a book that is no longer under the protection of copyright. The mash-up *Pride and Prejudice and Zombies* (2009) was published without legal fuss because the original Jane Austen books are no longer protected by copyright.

The Chilling Effects Clearinghouse (CEC) website is a joint project of the Electronic Frontier Foundation and the Harvard, Stanford, Berkeley, University of San Francisco, University of Maine, George Washington University, and Santa Clara University School of Law clinics. It addresses online activity and individuals' rights. It provides detailed information about copyright law and fan fiction, and anyone who is interested in the details of copyright law and fan activities should read through the site and the legal resources it recommends. In a nutshell, a fan fiction writer courts legal trouble through two avenues: (1) publishing and (2) distributing what they wrote. As the name of the Clearinghouse shows, the CEC is concerned that fear of copyright infringement could have a chilling effect on creativity. The CEC provides helpful guidance for avoiding that trouble while maintaining one's own rights.

LIBRARIANS AND FANDOM PROGRAMMING

Because fandom takes something personal (loving a story) and makes it public by building a community around that story, it is a great opportunity for libraries to tap into. This section will provide suggestions for library programming related to fandom.

Fan Writing Resources and Workshops

As described above, fan fiction writers can create works and receive appropriate guidance and feedback in their writing via fan networks. Questions about infringement are most likely to arise when it comes to publishing, distributing, or selling the work. So what can a library do? Libraries can create reference materials for writers and beta readers to use, and host workshops to teach fan writing and to make teens aware of possible legal issues.

It's important not to publish the fan fiction stories that result from these workshops, not on the library website, and not in a print collection to sell to raise money for the library. Instead, librarians should help writers find where they want to publish their work online at existing archives. You can read the various terms and conditions of those sites, find an established archive, and trust that the people running the archive know the ins and outs, such as which authors don't want fan fiction published online at all. You can also create online resources that link to places like the Chilling Effects Clearinghouse to provide fans with resources.

Fans like to analyze the works they love. Whether it's to dig and find deeper meaning, to try to reconcile a timeline covering multiple generations, or to predict what will happen in the future, fandom is about discussing a work and being able to back it up by citing a book title and page number. Because such essays usually comply with fair use (depending on how much of the original work is quoted), they can be published. A search of online booksellers for essays about *Twilight* results in a number of enticing possibilities, including *A New Dawn: Your Favorite Authors on Stephenie Meyer's Twilight Saga: Completely Unauthorized* (2008), edited by Ellen Hopkins.

Re-creation Events

The plots of many YA books include an important occasion or a memorable place: a prom, a dance, a party, a meal. These are the perfect types of events around which to build library programs. Teens can dress up as the characters, eat their favorite foods, play their music, and decorate the library to reflect the book's setting. For *Twilight*, it's a Twilight prom complete with photographs to imitate the famous "hands holding an apple" cover. *Harry Potter* offers plenty of ideas, from Tri-Wizard Tournaments to Yuletide Balls. Do you have fans of the Rick Riordan series about Percy Jackson? In the first book, *The Lightning Thief* (2005), Percy attends Camp Half-Blood. Why not host a Camp Half-Blood? If your readers are swooning over any historical book or historical fantasy set in Victorian or Edwardian times, the party is simple—an elegant tea party.

Fan Craft Programs

Fans often like to create fan items other than stories. Book-inspired crafts lend themselves especially well to library programming with teens. Any book can inspire craft ideas. Does the main character write in a journal? Have teens make their own journals. Does a particular item of jewelry figure into a plot? Schedule a jewelry making program. The programming possibilities are endless.

CONCLUSION

Today's online culture may at times seem overwhelming to those who don't participate, but it provides fans of books with the ability to find each other easily and to make connections based on shared passions. Those shared interests can result in creativity, thoughtful discourse, and just plain fun. Libraries can take advantage of teen fans' enthusiasm for books by promoting fandom via social networking and programming and, as a result, promoting the love of reading.

REFERENCES

Anderson, Laurie Halse. *Prom*. New York: Viking, 2005.
Austen, Jane, and Seth Grahame-Smith. *Pride and Prejudice and Zombies*. Philadelphia: Quirk Books, 2009.
Collins, Suzanne. *Hunger Games*. New York: Scholastic, 2008.
Eligon, John. "Rowling Wins Lawsuit Against Potter Lexicon." *The New York Times*, September 9, 2008, B3.

Garcia, Kami, and Margaret Stahl. *Beautiful Creatures*. New York: Little, Brown, 2009.

Hopkins, Ellen, ed. *A New Dawn: Your Favorite Authors on Stephenie Meyer's Twilight Saga: Completely Unauthorized*. Dallas: BenBella Books, 2008.

Hughes, Robert. "Return to the Range," *The Wall Street Journal*, September 6, 2008. http://online.wsj.com/article/SB122065020058105139.html/ (accessed February 19, 2010).

Hunter, Erin. *Into the Wild (Warriors Vol. 1)*. New York: HarperCollins, 2003.

Jacques, Brian. *Redwall*. New York: Philomel Books, 1986.

Lovelace, Mary Hart. *Betsy-Tacy*. New York: HarperCollins, 1940.

Meyer, Stephenie. *Breaking Dawn*. New York: Little Brown, 2008.

Meyer, Stephenie. *Twilight*. New York: Little, Brown, 2005.

Mitchell, Margaret. *Gone With the Wind*. New York: Macmillan, 1936.

Palahniuk, Chuck. *Fight Club*. New York: W.W. Norton & Company, 1996.

Randall, Alice. *The Wind Done Gone*. New York: Houghton Mifflin, 2001.

Riordan, Rick. *The Lightning Thief*. New York: Disney-Hyperion, 2005.

Smith, L. J. *The Vampire Diaries: The Awakening*. New York: HarperCollins, 2009.

Stiefvater, Maggie. *Shiver*. New York: Scholastic, 2009.

Turner, Megan Whalen. *A Conspiracy of Kings*. New York: HarperCollins, 2010.

Turner, Megan Whalen. *The Thief*. New York: Harper Collins, 1996.

Vander Ark, Steve. *The Lexicon: An Unauthorized Guide to Harry Potter Fiction and Related Materials*. Muskegon, MI: RDR Books, 2009.

Weiss, Sabrina Rojas, and Lisa Gonzalez. "*Breaking Dawn* Exclusive: *Twilight* Author Stephenie Meyer Reacts To Harsh Reader Complaints—'It Hurts.' "MTV.Com, August 8 2008, http://www.mtv.com/movies/news/articles/1592457/story.jhtml/ (accessed March 17, 2010).

Westerfeld, Scott. *Leviathan*. New York: Simon Pulse, 2009.

WEBSITES

Anderson, Laurie Halse. "About Contests and The Promises of Snow." Laurie Halse Anderson's Blog, February 6 2006, http://halseanderson.livejournal.com/72211.html/

Augustus, Sylvie. "Arthur Weasley's Relationship to Sirius Black: First Forays into the Black Family Tree." The Harry Potter Lexicon, http://www.hp-lexicon.org/essays/essay-black-family-tree.html/

Beautiful Creatures: A Novel by Kami Garcia and Margaret Stohl website, http://beautifulcreaturesthebook.com/

Beautiful Creatures Facebook page, http://www.facebook.com/pages/Beautiful-Creatures-the-Book/78607677903#/

Beautiful Creatures Ning, http://gatlincounty.ning.com/

Beautiful Creatures official publisher website, http://www.hachettebookgroup.com/features/somelovesarecursed/index.html/

Blue Trident website. "The No. 1 Fansite for Percy Jackson and the Olympians," http://www.bluetrident.org/

Camp Halfblood fansite, http://www.camphalfblood.blogspot.com/

The Caster Girls (& Boys), Official *Beautiful Creatures* Fansite, http://castergirls.com/

Chilling Effects Clearinghouse, http://www.chillingeffects.org/

Eddis, Attolia, Sounis, http://community.livejournal.com/sounis/

"The Essays." The Harry Potter Lexicon, http://www.hp-lexicon.org/essays/essay-index.html/

FanFiction.net, http://www.fanfiction.net/

FanFiction.net guidelines, www.fanfiction.net/guidelines/

FanFiction.net terms of service, www.fanfiction.net/tos/

Fiction Alley, http://www.fictionalley.org/

Glamourousgeek. "Merlin, God, and You-Know-Who: Religion in the Wizarding World." The Harry Potter Lexicon, http://www.hplex.info/essays/essay-religion-in-the-wizarding-world.html/

The Harry Potter Lexicon, http://www.hp-lexicon.org/

Houghton Mifflin court papers website, http://www.houghtonmifflinbooks.com/features/randall_url/courtpapers.shtml/

Hunger Games official Scholastic website, http://www.scholastic.com/thehungergames/

"Information About '*Suntrust Bank v. Houghton Mifflin Company* Court Papers.'" Houghton Mifflin Books website, http://www.houghtonmifflinbooks.com/features/randall_url/courtpapers.shtml/

Kami Garcia official website. http://kamimgarcia.typepad.com/

The Leaky Cauldron, http://www.the-leaky-cauldron.org/

LiveJournal. http://www.livejournal.com

Meg Cabot's Diary, www.megcabot.com

Margaret Stohl official website, http://www.margaretstohl.typepad.com/

"Memorable Quotes from *Fight Club* (1999)," IMDB Website, http://www.imdb.com/title/tt0137523/quotes/

"Michael L. Printz Award," American Library Association. http://www.ala.org/ala/mgrps/divs/yalsa/booklistsawards/printzaward/Printz.cfm/

MuggleNet. http://www.mugglenet.com/

"Rapunzel's Revenge Book Trailer Contest: Vote Now!" Squeetus Blog: Official Blog of Shannon Hale, February 8, 2010, http://oinks.squeetus.com/2010/02/rapunzels-revenge-book-trailer-contest-vote-now.html/

Redwall Wiki, http://redwall.wikia.com/wiki/Redwall_Wiki/

"Shiver." Maggie Stiefvater official website. http://www.maggiestiefvater.com/shiver.php/

"Shiver." Scholastic website, http://www2.scholastic.com/browse/book.jsp?id=1310712/

Stephenie Meyer's official website, http://www.stepheniemeyer.com/

Touched by *Twilight*, http://www.touchedbytwilight.net/

Twilight Lexicon, http://www.twilightlexicon.com/

Twilight Source, http://twilightsource.com/

Twilighted, http://www.twilighted.net/

TwilightMoms.com, http://www.twilightmoms.com/

U.S. Copyright Office, http://www.copyright.gov/

Vampire Diaries.Net, http://www.vampire-diaries.net/

Vander Ark, S., and B. Hobbs. About the Harry Potter Lexicon. 2009, http://www.hp-lexicon.org/help/lexicon.html#History/

Warner Bros. Entertainment Inc. et al. v. RDR Books et al. Justia.com News and Commentary, http://news.justia.com/cases/featured/new-york/nysdce/ 1:2007cv09667/315790/

The Warriors Encyclopedia. http://www.freewebs.com/the-warriors-encyclopedia/ index.htm/

10

◇ ◇ ◇

HANGING OUT ON THE GRID: VIRTUAL WORLDS FOR TEENS AND PRETEENS

Eric M. Meyers

In the 2009 film *Avatar*, directed by James Cameron, scientists have developed the capacity for humans to "drive" engineered hybrid bodies, called avatars, using their minds and sophisticated neural linking technology. In these avatar bodies, people are able to live, learn, and fall in love in an alien world, performing feats that their human bodies cannot. While the film is science fiction and the story takes place 150 years in the future, the idea of avatars as virtual representations of human minds and bodies is already here. Every day, millions of people log in to virtual worlds, where they interact with other participants via their avatars or 3D digital characters. They live, learn, fall in love, and do things they could not or would not do in the physical world. No science lab or exotic equipment is required; one only needs a modern computer and an Internet connection.

It is not surprising that teens are on the leading edge of virtual worlds (Virtual World News 2009). Having grown up online, teens and

This chapter was adapted in part from the paper "Tip of the Iceberg: Meaning, Identity, and Literacy in Preteen Virtual Worlds," presented at the Association for Library and Information Science Education (ALISE) Conference in Denver, Colorado, January 21, 2009.

tweens are active consumers of online services, and many possess the fearlessness, if not always the tech savvy, to engage with these technologies (Palfrey and Glasser 2008). Market research suggests that virtual worlds for youngsters are a key growth area: more new virtual worlds are being developed for users between ages 5 and 15 than for any other demographic, and the number of young people using these spaces far outnumbers users in the best-known adult worlds, such as Second Life. To give you a sense of scale, take one of the more popular teen virtual worlds, Habbo Hotel, which boasts 10 times the registered users of Second Life (KZero 2009). Researchers estimate that by 2011, over 50% of teen Internet users will be using virtual worlds to augment their online experiences (Williamson 2009).

Virtual worlds were originally envisioned as a physical apparatus to provide immersive experiences, either through a virtual reality (VR) "cave" or by using a helmet and goggles, much like the "holodeck" experience showcased in the *Star Trek* television series. Desktop VR, however, is run through personal computers, connecting users to landscapes, experiences, and each other via Web browsers. While not as immersive as VR caves or helmets, these virtual worlds offer everyday interactive experiences to the average Internet user (Castronova 2003). These more accessible virtual worlds, typified by Web spaces such as Teen Second Life, Habbo Hotel, and Gaia, are the topic of this chapter.

The popularity and ubiquity of virtual spaces for teens and tweens are not the only reasons to pay attention to them. Another reason is the role of virtual worlds in the way young people interact and communicate (Thomas and Brown 2009). Parents, teachers, and service providers are familiar with the plugged-in teen, ear buds in, seemingly disconnected from what is happening around her, immersed in her own digital world of music, video, and chat. Virtual worlds as immersive interactive spaces are facilitating the convergence of multiple media forms, making them a "one stop" social interactive venue. Teens can socialize with friends in real time, catch a live concert, or explore a digital replica of a famous museum—all within the same immersive application. Like the broader genre of social networking sites, virtual worlds do not replace the Web so much as they extend it in a fascinating new direction, one built on integrated experiences rather than discrete tasks or activities.

This chapter explores how virtual worlds fit into the larger framework of social networking for teens and young people. For those unfamiliar with virtual worlds, this chapter explains the features of several popular spaces and how these interactive worlds engage the social and developmental needs of youth. The chapter concludes with suggestions for librarians, educators, and information providers who wish to extend their services to teens into the virtual realm. Along the way, it grapples with several commonly asked questions:

- What are young people (and adults) doing in these online worlds?
- How are these worlds different from other social network technologies such as Facebook or MySpace?
- How can we understand virtual worlds in terms of youth learning and information-seeking behaviors to expand the youth services mission in schools and libraries?

GAMES OR VIRTUAL WORLDS?

I recently attempted to access several virtual worlds in a middle school computer lab, but the sites were blocked by the school's filtering mechanism. The reason, presented by the filter's autoresponder, was that these sites were categorized as games. Playing games is certainly part of the appeal of some virtual worlds, but I would argue that avatar-driven immersive sites like Teen Second Life (TSL) are far more than games. Furthermore, the "play" that children and adults engage in on these sites is beyond simple leisure. It would be easy to lump virtual worlds and online games into one category based on the use of avatars and rich, immersive landscapes, but that would deny some critical differences among these spaces: their purpose, the role of individual users in constructing meaning from their experiences with these virtual environments, as well as the transformation of these experiences through social interaction.

We often think of play as the realm of children, a leisure-time pursuit that they grow out of as they mature and move on to the serious business of being adults. Adults apply this same notion of play to youths' online spaces, considering them simple distractions or, worse yet, impediments to their cognitive and social development. Drawing on Salen and Zimmerman's seminal work on game design, we see an alternate perspective: they see play as the "free movement within a more rigid structure" (Salen and Zimmerman 2004, 306). In this sense, play represents the "possibility space" that exists within an activity system, the affordance among the constraints of social practice (Bogost 2008, 120). As youngsters play within virtual worlds, they are anything but distracted. Watching them navigate within these worlds, we see intense concentration as they negotiate meanings, solve problems, and explore the possibilities presented to their real/ virtual selves.

Virtual worlds have been conflated with massively multiplayer online role-playing games (MMORPGs) such as World of Warcraft (WoW) or EverQuest (EQ). This is due in part to the history of virtual worlds, which grew out of the role-playing game. Some of the earlier desktop VR applications were designed as first-person shooter games, merging online interactivity with the fictional setups of sophisticated console games. If, however, we define a game, as Salen and Zimmerman do, as "a system in which players engage in an artificial conflict, defined by rules, that results in a quantifiable outcome" (2004, 80), then WoW and EQ clearly fit the description of a game. TSL, on the other hand, does not.

Furthermore, virtual worlds lack the strong story lines and graded progressions (levels) that are present in MMORPGs. But it is not just what virtual worlds lack that makes them different. Virtual worlds are massively multiuser spaces that permit collaboration and social interaction in real time around the unique story lines of their participants. The meaning that is created in these spaces is distinct and validated by the social actors themselves rather than predetermined by the game designers. In this sense, virtual worlds for youngsters share more in common with collaborative spaces such as There or Second Life than video games. The bottom line is that games are more than leisure, and virtual worlds are more than just games. The purpose of virtual worlds, then, is to create a canvas for user-generated interaction rather than a scripted story arc in which the users are mere participants.

TWEEN AND TEEN VIRTUAL WORLDS: AN EMERGENT GENRE

The last 3 years have seen a dramatic increase in the number of online virtual spaces targeting the preteen or tween (ages 7 to 12) and teen (ages 13 to 18) demographics as well as the Internet traffic directed to these sites. It is estimated that over 10 million youths and adults use these sites in North America and around the world, and that figure is growing (Williamson 2009). The virtual spaces are also becoming more diverse as developers see new opportunities to engage new participants and younger Internet users. Many of these sites are so new that we have little research evidence to draw on for guidance. Table 10.1 provides a short list of popular virtual worlds that target a teen audience.

Table 10.1: Examples of Preteen, Teen, and Adult Virtual Worlds

	Preteen Worlds			Teen Worlds			Adult Worlds
	Club Penguin	Barbie Girls	Whyville	Gaia	Habbo Hotel	Teen Second Life	Second Life
URL	Clubpenguin.com	Barbiegirls.com	Whyville.net	Gaiaonline.com	Habbo.com	Secondlife.com	Secondlife.com
Premise	Create a penguin character; play games; decorate an igloo; engage in adventures; chat with friends.	Create, dress, and style a Barbie character; host virtual parties; play games; chat with friends.	Educational world designed around participation in learning activities.	Anime-focused social world with discussion boards, virtual spaces, e-mail, chat, guilds.	Own your own room in a virtual hotel, hang out with friends, chat, shop for goods with real money.	Create a 3D "resident"; build content; engage in activities; chat with friends.	Create a 3D "resident"; build content; engage in activities; chat with friends.
Target audience	Ages 6–14	Girls Ages 7–13	Ages 11–15	Ages 13–18	Ages 13–18	Ages 13–17	Adults
Avatar	Anthropomorphic penguin	Barbie girl character	Hand-drawn human character	Anime human character	"Habbo" human character	3D Character	3D Character
Point of view	Birdseye view, 2D sprite	Birdseye view, 2D sprite	Birdseye view, 2D sprite	Birdseye view, 2D sprite	Birdseye view, 2D sprite	First person, over shoulder	First person, over shoulder
Parent information	Yes	Yes	Yes	Yes	Yes	Yes	N/A
Unique monthly visitors*	2,872,383	646,361	33,360	1,001,862	245,716	~50,000	276,223
Total monthly visits*	16,086,723	1,225,061	67,675	6,372,231	786,541	Not available	954,970
Revenue sources	Premium membership, merchandise	Premium membership, merchandise	Nonprofit; research grants, corporate partnerships	Advertisements, premium membership, merchandise	Advertisements, premium membership, merchandise	Advertisements, land sales, premium membership	Advertisements, land sales, premium membership

*Figures are for November 2009, gathered from Compete.com (2009)

What we know already is that virtual worlds are not a one-size-fits-all category, even if they have many closely related features. As the market for virtual worlds has increased in recent years and as the age range of users expands, virtual world developers are striving to provide a unique experience while maintaining a sufficiently low bar for entry. Second Life, with its rich set of features and extensive customizability, is closer to a blank canvas than worlds designed for younger and less experienced users. We can see a clear separation between the worlds designed for both young children and tweens (ages 4 to 12) and those with a teen audience in mind (ages 13 and up), both in terms of the look and feel of the sites and the features that are available to users.

Tween virtual worlds, such as Club Penguin, EcoBuddies, and Web-Kinz, are designed for the youngest users, ages 4 and up. They allow children to create an avatar that they move through the various spaces (islands, rooms, neighborhoods) represented in the world. The avatars, as well as the homes or rooms, can be decorated with a wide array of furnishings and accessories. A dashboard of simple controls and a moderated chat system allow for simple manipulation of avatars and communication options. Playing games or engaging in various adventures scripted within the world permits children to earn virtual currency, which can be spent on additional virtual accessories, clothing, and furniture.

Much of the activity in these worlds appears to be consumer-oriented; children spend a great deal of their time shopping or working/playing in order to afford more virtual possessions. The goal is to provide an entry-level, readily enjoyable experience with a shallow learning curve. That said, tweens and teens are present in worlds like Club Penguin, but they are drawn more to the chat capabilities than the games. They have been known to use the penguin avatars for creative purposes, such as machinima, which are videos using game or virtual world avatars to act out movie scenes or music videos. An example of this type of creativity, with over a million views on YouTube, is "Bad Day in Club Penguin" by Tehkraziboi. The original video has been removed, but it spawned numerous imitations, including dozens of "puffle" music videos (e.g., Puffles singing "Do you like waffles?"). Virtual worlds targeting older children and teens have a more sophisticated look, greater customizability, and features that demand more skill. Instead of avatars that represent anthropomorphic animals (penguins in Club Penguin, cats in HandiPoints, hamsters in EcoBuddies), the avatars are more likely to look human. Barbie Girls, Gaia, Habbo, and TSL all use hominid avatars, even if the fidelity of these characters varies significantly (some more pixilated that others) and may be customized with nonhuman features such as wings, tails, skins, and so on. Users are encouraged to develop a style that represents the user rather than a generic form. On Gaia, for example, users are prompted to create a "look" for their avatars: "On Gaia, you define your look: be quirky, cute, scary, heroic or even nerdy. It's all up to you" (Gaia Online 2010).

With an increase in the fidelity of the virtual experience, teen sites offer increased communication options as well. The chat capability is more like a nonsequential group conversation than an instant message interface, and there are fewer preprogrammed words and phrases ("Hi! Want to be friends?") than one sees in worlds for young children. Some worlds integrate games, discussion forums, and organization structures (clubs, guilds, affinity groups). All include the ability to develop friend lists or to find people with similar interests. These virtual spaces incorporate many of the features found in social networking applications such as Facebook or MySpace. One of the key differences is the inclusion of an interactive "space" where participants interact in real time using their avatars.

Teen Second Life (TSL) is arguably the most sophisticated offering among virtual worlds designed for young people. TSL uses the same technology and rendering engine as the adult space, but it is a separate grid exclusively for teens and select adults. The purpose is to keep younger users from the mature content found on the adult grid as well as to give teens a safe, private space away from adults. In TSL, users have greater freedom to develop content, sell their own creations (jewelry, clothing, and other artifacts), and rent land to build their own virtual homes or shops. This sophistication comes at a price, however: the learning curve for TSL is just as steep as adult Second Life. As a result, TSL, for all its promise, has significantly fewer users than worlds like Gaia, which have a much lower bar for entry.

Two key concerns for all virtual spaces designed expressly for youth are user privacy and anonymity. This is more explicit in the worlds designed for younger children, which enforce chat norms that prevent the disclosure of personal information and discourage the use of real identities in the creation of user names and profiles. As a result of these protection features, adults can and are even encouraged to use young children's virtual worlds as a means of facilitating intergenerational play (e.g., grandparents can play in Club Penguin with their grandchildren without traveling to visit them).

This is not the case with worlds targeted to teens. These spaces are considered for young people only. This is made explicit in the registration process and user agreements. Because the focus of teen worlds is less on play and more on socialization and shared experience, these sites do not wish to have mixed generational interaction. TSL, for instance, explains in its user agreement that it is for youths aged 13 to 17 only. Furthermore, the agreement indicates that Linden Lab will inform law enforcement should adults attempt to register using false birth dates. This creates concerns for parents and service providers who wish to moderate and scaffold behavior in these spaces. There are, however, exceptions to this, as discussed in a later section.

THE DIFFERENCE THAT SPACE MAKES

Facebook uses the metaphor of an interactive college yearbook to connect users and facilitate interactions. Virtual worlds for teens, on the other hand, use spatial metaphors to emphasize the immersive nature of users' activities. Habbo Hotel, for instance, using a hotel metaphor, is like a college dormitory community. Teens not only customize their avatars (called Habbos), selecting clothes, accessories, skin, hairstyle, and eye color, but also their rooms. They can select furniture, wall, and floor coverings to make the room feel like "home." For socialization purposes, Habbos can have a guest room or invite friends over for a party. By utilizing the spatial metaphor, the site invites creative fantasy about the activities of adults, including control over their surroundings, and supports teens' developmental needs (Beals and Bers 2009).

Chatting, friending, sharing artifacts, and game play with other teens are features that make virtual worlds similar to social networks. What makes them unique is the sense of space that facilitates new perspectives and types of interaction among users. I see four key differences between virtual worlds and social networks: (1) synchronous communication; (2) social presence; (3) exploration; and 4) creation. These four differences are explained below.

1. **Synchronous communication:** In sharing a virtual environment, you interact with users—many users, if you like—in real time. You can converse with groups of users instead of a single person. This is a significant step beyond the individual, sequential interaction one experiences with a Facebook profile, where comments are made one by one and conversations accumulate over hours or days.

2. **Sense of social presence:** When other users are online, you see not only indications that they are logged in but also their avatars, which appear on the computer screen, where you can interact

with them. Experiences are shared in different ways and make the quality of multiuser interactions richer and, in many ways, more fulfilling than other kinds of Web-enabled collaboration.

3. **Exploration:** Virtual worlds are presented as a "space" that unfolds as the user views and examines it from the point of view of the avatar. Some worlds offer a first-person or over-the-shoulder viewpoint while others provide a simple birds-eye view of the landscape. Either way, this ability to explore a changing landscape leads to more opportunities, more configurations, and a greater sense of possibility. What the user sees is unique, compelling, and ultimately more immersive.

4. **Creation:** Virtual worlds are places where creative agency is both facilitated and rewarded. While the ability of users to generate content varies on the sophistication of the software used to render each world, the incorporation of user content is one of the distinguishing factors of these spaces as a collaborative venture between designers and users.

Social networking sites are often critiqued for the permanence and searchability of their contents; a teen who posts images or comments on MySpace may find these vestiges of younger days affecting college admissions, job interviews, or relationships. This is one of the ways that the synchronous and more anonymous interactions in virtual worlds differ. The sense of presence and point of view means that there is a great deal of localized, ephemeral interaction in these spaces that is not recorded and preserved for the public or for other users. Furthermore, the barriers between virtual world users and nonusers make data less accessible to the general public.

WHO ARE YOU? BUILDING AN ONLINE IDENTITY

It is common to hear people discuss virtual activities with physical world counterparts, or the lack thereof, by using the terms *virtual life* or *second life* in contrast to *real life*. It would be disingenuous, however, to suggest that what happens in virtual worlds is not "real." Indeed, there are real consequences to activities in virtual space. Teens and tweens invest time, effort, and emotion in virtual worlds and the avatars they customize to represent their styles and self-perceptions.

We view the teen years as an important formative period but also one of uncertainty. During this period, young people forge aspects of their personalities, styles of interaction with peers, and sense of who they are in relation to others. They are experimenting with different identities, including physical appearance, social configurations, roles, and interactions (Wigfield et al. 2006). Virtual worlds can facilitate these experiments by providing a different audience than the home or school environment as well as tools to shift and shape identity features with lower costs (both in terms of monetary costs and social costs, such as embarrassment). A person can try out being Goth one day and Preppy the next, simply by changing the appearance of his or her avatar. It is possible to develop multiple identities online, with different friend groups and outward appearances, cultivating, testing, and discarding different personalities.

Virtual worlds may also provide a safe space for teens who do not fit in well with the majority of their peers in school or the local community. Students with social stigmas in the physical world can develop an online identity unconstrained by the social pressures of everyday acquaintances. The emergence of virtual support groups for adults suggests that a sense of belonging and community can be fostered through online interactions, particularly when avatars are not affected by the physical constraints that can be present in one's everyday life, including appearance, social awkwardness, and disability, to name a few. By making distance a nonissue, virtual connections can foster community for those who have limited mobility or live in areas of low population density.

While the freedom to engage in identity play is an empowering aspect of virtual worlds, there are challenges that can constrain users. From evidence on blogs and parent forums, the commercial or noncommercial nature of a given virtual world appears to be an important factor to both parents and teen users. It dramatically affects the extent to which users can participate in the activities offered in these spaces. Sites that offer premium membership ($6 to $10 per month) often reserve many activities for those who subscribe at this level. As membership is reflected in the appearance of a user's avatar in the world or in the extent to which users can customize their rooms or acquire items—very often the symbols of status and belonging—there is tremendous social pressure to pay these premiums. Most offer a "free" base-level subscription, but even Teen Second Life, which is free so long as you do not purchase or upload content, requires a PayPal account during registration. For teens who do not have a source of income or parents who are willing to support membership, this can be a serious barrier to participation.

A NEW WAY OF LOOKING AT ONLINE SOCIALIZING

On the surface, virtual worlds appear to be the center of a lot of chatting, gaming, and consumer-oriented behavior. This is certainly the case with many social networking sites and virtual worlds, both for adults and youth. But in watching these sites over the course of many months, I have also found these worlds to be the focus of a great deal of information work, not only within the virtual space but more impressively outside of it. This work was evident in information seeking as well as information building in the creation of fan pages, blogs, walkthroughs, and machinima videos. The four points below help describe what I observed, like a lens through which I analyzed teens' online activity—a set of virtual world goggles, if you will.

Virtual World as Identity Space

We express ourselves by how we dress, the car we drive, or the type of house we live in. Through participation in virtual worlds, teens are given the chance to develop a persona—a unique identity that reflects their growing sense of self. The flexibility to create a personal (malleable and disposable) online style that mimics or contradicts the physical self offers teens an opportunity for low-stakes identity play. This projection of the real self in virtual space has tremendous potential for learning and could be a building block in the construction of the social self (Thomas and Brown 2009). Librarians can approach identity play as a teachable moment for developing online habits and cybercitizenship. It can also serve as a jumping-off point for discussing notions of authority, credibility, trust, and the social costs of peer information sharing.

Virtual World as New Literacy

As teens and tweens engage with virtual spaces, they participate in a discourse community with rules, norms, and a system that requires learning (Kress 2003; Steinkuehler 2008). Logging in, creating an avatar, chatting, and sharing an online profile with others are skills and literacies that transfer across multiple applications.

There are two new things that make virtual worlds exciting as a new kind of literacy. First is the ability for teens to engage with websites and each other in novel ways, from social networking and chat, to creating and manipulating customizable avatars, to building and developing artifacts for others to use. While these technologies have been around for some time, placing them in the hands of youngsters in a developmentally appropriate way is the important innovation (Knobel and Lankshear 2006).

The second exciting thing is the manner in which teens are engaging with these spaces, specifically moving from knowledge consumers (decoding the text of others) to knowledge producers (demonstrating expertise through weblogs, fan sites, and videos). Teens are the experts in these spaces, even if the spaces are created and/or moderated by adults. In many ways, these sites are like boot camp for the online activities that we now consider essential to information literacy and technological fluency. To support these activities, librarians, among others, need to expand their notion of what it means to be literate. This demands that we move beyond decoding and encoding text to recognizing that print literacy is an essential starting point rather than an ending point. The capacity to engage and flourish intellectually in the digital realm requires multiple interrelated literacies (Gee 2008).

Virtual World as Problem-Solving Contexts

People continually engage in information problem solving—identifying needs, selecting sources, determining credibility and relevance, and making decisions or drawing conclusions. Information problem solving is particularly relevant in immersive virtual environments, where new tools are providing users with novel ways of using, interpreting, and sharing information. There are very few instructions in many of these spaces; teens often immerse themselves in the space and begin solving in-world issues of navigation, personalization, and communication right away. As their comfort level with the world increases, it appears that the problems switch emphasis, from solving problems about being in the virtual world (How do I do that?) to solving everyday problems in the world (What homework do we have in math?). These are information problems, and as such, young people can and should be looking at problem solving models like the Big6 to scaffold their process (Eisenberg 2008). Educators and librarians can help them make this connection. Research on information provision in Second Life (Mon 2009) documents how adult reference services can provide a unique opportunity to connect with virtual world users. Beyond ready reference, virtual worlds provide the capacity to explore problems from different angles, test ideas, and engage in role-play that might not be available in physical world settings.

Another way in which virtual information spaces can facilitate problem solving is by providing a safe, anonymous place to ask questions users may be hesitant to ask in person. By extending information services to avatar-based interaction, librarians can overcome some of the barriers that hamper outreach to sensitive young people, particularly with regard to health and wellness issues, thus minimizing the social costs of information seeking.

Virtual Worlds as Communities

Virtual spaces offer synchronous interaction within the world—opportunities to play and socialize with others—as well as points of asynchronous interaction online through fan sites, weblogs, and YouTube videos. What emerges is a sense of community, a membership in a larger enterprise in which other youth participate. In many ways, the teens and tweens in virtual worlds become a community of practice, one that shapes their understanding of the online world and their identities as members. Beyond the plethora of "hacks" and "cheats" identified by users, websites offer instruction and insight from experienced members, detailed tutorials on how to earn rewards, and techniques that novices can employ to improve their standing in the community. As educators, we often strive to make our classrooms communities of learners. This type of community has emerged spontaneously online in response to shared virtual experiences. The keys appear to be motivation and agency: finding activities that young people enjoy and giving them the agency to demonstrate their expertise in multiple modalities. Librarians regularly reach out to the community by offering programming geared to the needs of specific user groups. This type of outreach may also be effective in youth virtual communities.

This framework as a whole identifies the purposes these worlds fulfill as well as the ways in which we might find connections among virtual activities and analogs in the physical world. Each point presents an opportunity to look at these spaces and imagine new possibilities for teen services.

DEVELOPING VIRTUAL SERVICES: OPPORTUNITIES AND CHALLENGES

Librarians have been working in Second Life and other virtual worlds for several years, creating sophisticated outreach displays, reference collections, and spaces like InfoIsland in Second Life to support a variety of information needs and challenges (Mon 2009). For virtual worlds, services can come in three varieties: (1) in-world presence for reference and referral, (2) in-world programming on topics of interest, and (3) out-world support for in-world activities.

In-world presence is the most high-profile way libraries can deliver services in virtual worlds. It is also the most expensive and challenging to maintain over time. Developing an "island" in TSL, for example, requires monthly land-use fees and the investment of hundreds or thousands of hours constructing the virtual space using the buildings blocks of SL, called prims. Without experience with this system, the undertaking would call for more than most libraries would wish to invest, both in terms of time and money. Even leveraging the talents of teens to "terraform" and maintain a space would be a significant investment.

In adult Second Life, the Alliance Library System (ALS) integrated the efforts of dozens of librarians and service providers to create InfoIsland. This type of alliance was also attempted on the teen grid, with partners ALS and the Public Library of Charlotte Mecklenburg County (PLCMC) in North Carolina. The resulting Eye4You project on the teen grid went live in 2006, but it had to close down its virtual presence in the summer of 2009. During the 3 years it was on the grid, the Eye4You Alliance provided in-world homework help, teen programming, and literacy engagement activities with TSL residents (Eye4You Alliance). Several education projects maintain a presence in TSL, including Global Kids, which has a wealth of advice for service providers who want to develop spaces for teens in virtual worlds.

One of the challenges posed by the provision of space and services in-world is gaining access and credibility. As mentioned previously, many sites for teens restrict adult access, prompting adults to apply for permission. Librarians must respect this restriction by associating with an educational or outreach institution that provides needed services, training, or enrichment activities to youth. Gaining access to the virtual world, however, is only the first step. Building credibility requires engaging with residents or users, participating in activities as an avatar, and demonstrating value to youth. These efforts take time and necessitate collaboration with young people in the design and implementation of services. Most importantly, librarians must listen to youth voices and recognize when the young know best.

A more basic but still worthwhile approach to supporting teens in virtual worlds is developing an understanding of these spaces and providing the physical and technical access teens need to participate. Not every service provider will create an in-world presence, nor will every librarian be comfortable as a digitized avatar providing cyberbased homework help. But cultivating a knowledgeable, tech savvy youth services team that can provide reference and assistance from the outside is also valuable. Furthermore, not every teen will be supported from home in accessing these spaces. High-speed connections and modern computers, which many libraries provide, can give less privileged youth the opportunity to extend their online activities and gain new skills and digital literacies. This type of support demands an orientation toward virtual spaces that is positive and encouraging, recognizing the social and developmental benefits that draw tweens and teens to these sites.

CONCLUSION

Rapid improvements in computing technology have brought the wonders of "synthetic worlds" into the homes of millions of Americans (Castronova 2003). This is not science fiction; virtual environments are quickly becoming an important aspect of young people's out-of-school lives (Marsh 2008; Merchant 2009; Meyers 2009). However, little empirical research documents these spaces or the techniques that researchers might employ to study them. Also lacking are solid, sustained models of library practice that actively reaches out to youth communities in virtual worlds. These spaces offer tremendous potential to engage youth in a medium to which they are drawn socially and experientially.

Many youth service departments have adopted Facebook, MySpace, and Twitter, among other social networking technologies, to connect with teen audiences, advertise programs, and provide ready reference and homework assistance. These types of activities can also be supported in virtual spaces, but with greater fidelity of interaction, real-time communication, and immersive simulations. Virtual worlds incorporate many of the features of social networking applications while also providing rich opportunities for collaboration and learning, which take online interaction to the next level. As more teens and tweens enter virtual worlds, librarians and service providers should consider reaching out to the youngsters on the grid.

REFERENCES

Beals, Laura, and Marina U. Bers. "A Developmental Lens for Designing Virtual Worlds for Children and Youth." *International Journal of Learning and Media* 1, no. 1 (2009): 51–65.

Bogost, Iain. "The Rhetoric of Video Games." In *The Ecology of Games: Connecting Youth, Games, and Learning,* edited by Katie Salen, 117–40. The John D. and Catherine T. MacArthur Foundation Series on Digital Media and Learning. Cambridge, MA: MIT Press, 2008.

Cameron, James, dir. *Avatar.* Twentieth Century Fox, 2009. Film.

Castronova, Edward. *Synthetic Worlds: The Business and Culture of Online Games.* Chicago: University of Chicago Press, 2003.

Compete.com. "Site Profile Search," http://siteanalytics.compete.com/ (accessed December 28, 2009).

Eisenberg, Michael B. "Information Literacy: Essential Skills for the Information Age." *DESIDOC Journal of Library & Information Technology* 28, no. 2 (2008): 39–47.

EverQuest. Sony Online Entertainment (SOE), 1999. Game.

Eye4You Alliance, http://eye4youalliance.youthtech.info/ (accessed January 30, 2010).

Gaia Online, http://www.gaiaonline.com/ (accessed January 30, 2010).

Gee, James P. "Getting Over the Slump: Innovation Strategies to Promote Children's Learning." White paper prepared for the Joan Ganz Cooney Center, 2008, http://www.joanganzcooneycenter.org/pdf/Cooney_policy_0506.pdf/ (accessed January 30, 2010).

Knobel, Michele, and Colin Lankshear. "Sampling the 'New' in New Literacies." In *A New Literacies Sampler,* edited by Michele Knobel and Colin Lankshear. New York: Peter Lang, 2006.

Kress, Gunther. *Literacy in the New Media Age.* London: Routledge, 2003.

KZero Research. "The Virtual Worlds Radar," http://www.kzero.co.uk/radar.php/ (accessed September 25, 2009).

Marsh, Jackie. "Out-of-School Play in Online Virtual Worlds and the Implications for Literacy Learning." Paper presented at the Centre for Studies in Literacy, Policy and Learning Cultures, University of South Australia, 2008, http://www.unisa.edu.au/hawkeinstitute/cslplc/documents/JackieMarsh.pdf/ (accessed November 28, 2009).

Merchant, Guy. "Literacy in Virtual Worlds." *Journal of Research in Reading* 32, no. 1 (2009): 38–56.

Meyers, Eric M. "Tip of the Iceberg: Meaning, Identity, and Literacy in Preteen Virtual Worlds." *Journal of Education for Library and Information Science* 50, no. 4 (2009): 232–42.

Mon, Lori. "Questions and Answers in a Virtual World: Educators and Librarians as Information Providers in Second Life." *Journal of Virtual World Research* 2, no. 1 (2009): 3–21.

Palfrey, John, and Urs Gasser. *Born Digital: Understanding the First Generation of Digital Natives.* New York: Basic Books, 2008.

Salen, Katie, and Eric Zimmerman. *Rules of Play: Game Design Fundamentals.* Cambridge, MA: MIT Press, 2004.

Steinkuehler, Constance A. "Cognition and Literacy in Massively Multiplayer Online Games." In *Handbook of Research on New Literacies,* edited by Julie Coiro, Michele Knobel, Colin Lankshear, and Donald J. Leu, 611–34. New York: Lawrence Erlbaum Associates, 2008.

Thomas, Douglas, and John Seely Brown. "Why Virtual Worlds Matter." *International Journal of Learning and Media* 1, no. 1 (2009): 37–49.

Virtual World News. "Teen and Preteen Migration to Virtual Worlds on the Rise." May 21, 2009, http://www.virtualworldsnews.com/2009/05/teen-preeteen-migration-to-virtual-worlds-on-the-rise.html/ (accessed November 28, 2009).

Wigfield, Allan, James P. Byrnes, and Jacquelynne S. Eccles. "Development During Early and Middle Adolescence." In *Handbook of Educational Psychology,* 2nd ed., edited by Patricia A. Alexander and Philip H. Winne, 87–114. Mahwah, NJ: Lawrence Erlbaum, 2006.

Williamson, Debra A. "Real Kids in Virtual Worlds." *eMarketer,* May 21, 2009, http://www.emarketer.com/Article.aspx?R=1007095/ (accessed November 28, 2009).

WEBSITES

BarbieGirls.com, http://barbiegirls.com/
Club Penguin, http://clubpenguin.com/
EcoBuddies, http://eccobuddies.com/
EverQuest, everquest.com/
Global Kids, www.holymeatballs.org/
Habbo Hotel, http://www.habo.com/
HandiPoints, http://www.handipoints.com/

Puffle music video, see http://www.youtube.com/watch?v=Pfex-ISPaRo/
Second Life, www.secondlife.com/
Teen Second Life. Linden Lab, http://teen.secondlife.com/ (accessed February 20, 2010).
There, www.there.com/
WebKinz, http://www.webkinz.com/
World of Warcraft, worldofwarcraft.com/

11

PAGES, PROFILES, AND PODCASTS: HOW CHARLOTTE MECKLENBURG LIBRARY ENGAGES TEENS THROUGH SOCIAL NETWORKING

Holly Summers, Rebecca Pierson, Christen Higgins, and Ralph Woodring

Charlotte Mecklenburg Library (nicknamed "the Library") is one of the nation's leading library systems and has been operating for over 100 years. Currently, the Library maintains 24 branch locations, including ImaginOn: The Joe and Joan Martin Center. In 2006, it was awarded the National Medal for Library Service by the Institute for Museum and Library Services. In addition, the Library received the highest possible rating of five stars from the *Library Journal*'s Index of Public Library Service in both 2009 and 2010. With a mission of expanding minds, empowering individuals, and enriching the community, the Library continues to set milestones in the library world.

The Teen Services Division at Charlotte Mecklenburg Library employs 35 staff members dedicated to planning, implementing, and evaluating outstanding and developmentally appropriate services for all teens ages 12 through 18. Each branch has at least one teen specialist on staff, although some branches have two or more. Over the course of 10 years, these staff members as well as dedicated staff from other departments have implemented the various social networking tools that the Library uses and benefits from today.

Michele Gorman has been coordinating Charlotte Mecklenburg Library's teen services since her arrival in 2005. Under her leadership, teen specialists are encouraged to fearlessly but deliberately explore new services for and with teens. While many libraries face obstacles with providing social networking technologies, staff at the Library are supported and challenged to try new things. The pursuit of innovation as a means of keeping services and technology contemporary and vibrant is a focal point of the Library's core values.

At the forefront of teen services, especially with regard to social networking technologies, is ImaginOn, a collaborative venture between Charlotte Mecklenburg Library and the Children's Theatre of Charlotte. This nationally recognized facility serves both children and teens through extraordinary experiences that challenge, inspire, and excite young minds. The Loft at ImaginOn, a library space exclusively for teens ages 12 through 19, and Tech Central, a technology-driven area equipped with over 30 computers, promote digital and visual literacy for teens through the use of technology. It is here that many social networking tools are first implemented, serving as a testing ground for services that are eventually used systemwide.

Teens gather at the Loft @ ImaginOn, a space in the Charlotte Mecklenburg Library system created exclusively for young people.

With a knowledgeable and dedicated teen services staff and leader, ample technological resources, and an award-winning organizational philosophy that values innovation and accessibility, the Library has created an ideal environment for exploring social networking as a tool for connecting with teen patrons. This chapter describes our experiences of social networking with teens and shares the lessons we've learned from those experiences.

LOGGING IN: HOW CHARLOTTE MECKLENBURG LIBRARY FIRST EMBRACED SOCIAL NETWORKING

Social networking is now a daily practice at Charlotte Mecklenburg Library, but our adoption of social media was a gradual and experimental process. On many fronts, we have only recently found a real connection with teens within the social networking landscape, and there are still more methods yet to be used or even considered. In fact, our first venture into social media was not related to teen services at all.

Blogs

In 2006, the Library encouraged its staff to create their own blogs as a part of its Learning 2.0 initiative. It was here that social media were first embraced and tested at Charlotte Mecklenburg Library, allowing various staff members—whether involved in teen services or not—to discuss library-related issues in an online forum. Podcasting was also implemented around this time, occasionally being used as a part of the "Monday Memo" program, a weekly e-mail release for the purpose of updating library staff on current library news. Seeing how clearly and effectively such tools could connect with fellow staff, we began looking for ways to apply these ideas toward connecting with patrons.

MySpace

This led to our first use of social media specifically for teen services. It began in April 2006 when the Loft at ImaginOn introduced a MySpace page. "We were influenced by practicality," says former Loft staff member Jesse Vieau. "Teenagers came to The Loft to use our computers to check their own social networking pages. As staff, we had to learn how the sites worked so we could help the teens troubleshoot and offer more options"

(Vieau 2009). By watching computer usage trends and speaking with patrons, the staff saw how enthusiastic teens were about using social networking. It was only logical to expand the Library's services to the more popular social networking websites.

After consulting with teen patrons as to whether and how they'd use a library MySpace page, the staff of The Loft created one, making sure to incorporate teen input about the look, structure, and content of the page. With this new social networking presence, The Loft was now able to connect with teens and other patrons in an entirely different way, educating them about the library and providing news about its many activities. "MySpace was a great success for us from the beginning, helping us promote our programs to more than 1,000 local teens and helping us establish or continue building relationships with [teens], both those who had spent time in our library and those who had never been inside our buildings" (Gorman 2009).

The Loft's MySpace page was instrumental in spreading the word to Charlotte teens about the very existence of ImaginOn and The Loft: "There wasn't even a sign on the front of the building, but we did have a Web presence in the networks teens were already using. That made them come to our URL to find us" (Vieau 2009). Since its creation, the Loft's MySpace page has continued to expand its friend list and offer updates on a regular basis. In an effort to attract patrons, several library-related features were added to the page. The Loft's MySpace page includes an iPac widget created by the Library's web services department that allows teens to search the library catalog from MySpace. In addition, Studio i, ImaginOn's multimedia production studio for children and teens, provides lots of teen-created content for the MySpace page, from the videos that are posted to the music that plays when users land on the page (Vieau 2010).

In response to the Loft's MySpace popularity, individual branches began creating their own pages in order to attract patrons. "After we used The Loft's page as our guinea pig to work out the kinks and understand how and why we would use [MySpace], we then encouraged other branches to create their own, and it took off from there" (Vieau 2009).

Creating Official Standards

To encourage consistency and help staff across the library system create developmentally appropriate pages for teens, in 2006 the staff at The Loft created official standards for library MySpace pages. These standards ensured that Charlotte Mecklenburg Library's MySpace pages represented the Library rather than any specific individual creating the pages. They included guidelines, such as consistent tagging ("Charlotte," "library," "teens," etc.) and restrictions to friend requests (only accepting teens, other libraries/librarians, local youth-serving organizations, and young adult [YA] authors). A *Parent's Handbook* explaining MySpace's purpose and the Library's involvement with the social network was also created in 2006. Both the official standards and the *Parent's Handbook* include the Federal Trade Commission's "Social Networking Sites: Safety Tips for Tweens and Teens" (2006).

By creating personalized MySpace pages, branches were able to update interested patrons on news and events exclusive to each location. Testing these services at The Loft and providing guidelines for them not only gave Charlotte Mecklenburg Library's branch libraries a framework to start with but also provided reassurance for branch staff and supervisors who might have been uncertain about trying something new. "I think once we started promoting social networking tools as legitimate tools for connecting with teens, other libraries within the system felt like they had the go-ahead and administrative support to give it a try in their locations" (Gorman 2009).

Meebo

We also saw the introduction of Meebo as a means for directly communicating with patrons at the Loft in 2006. A Meebo wigdet on the Library's teen website, LibraryLoft, allows users to easily send an instant message (IM) to the library without having to log in to a separate IM service. Now teens could not only look online for library promotion but also ask questions and offer feedback directly to the library staff. "Meebo is really successful because it allows people to quickly ask us questions about something they see on our website while they are looking at our website," says Amy Wyckoff (2009), teen librarian at The Loft. The majority of questions encountered on Meebo are from teens looking for books or other library resources, especially at the end of summer when they are looking for school reading lists. Meebo is also a popular way for teen patrons to ask questions about how the Teen Summer Reading program works or to find out details about the Teen Read Week Party.

Flickr and YouTube

With the success of MySpace and Meebo, The Loft began looking for other ways of connecting with patrons online. This time, more visual uses of social media were pursued by creating Flickr and YouTube accounts. Flickr was an ideal way to share the multitudes of photos of teen events at the library. Browsing the Library's Flickr stream, teens can not only learn what kinds of programs are offered by all of the branches but also find pictures of themselves and their friends if they've attended a program. Allowing teens to view pictures of themselves and their friends or class-mates helps them to feel involved with their library and connected to their community, which affects teens positively on many levels.

Similarly, a shared teen services YouTube account offered the ability to show patrons, frame for frame, teen events and teen-created content online. Both Flickr and YouTube were quickly embraced. To this day they continue to provide a stream of photos and videos for patrons and staff alike.

Second Life

Also in 2006, the Library was experimenting with virtual interactiv-ity on the Web with the creation of a Second Life island named Eye-4YouAlliance. This project was led by Kelly Czarnecki, technology education librarian at ImaginOn. Founded through a partnership with the Alliance Library System (ALS), an original island within Second Life offered a host of new ways for teens and other patrons to interact with the library. The project involved many librarians, educators, and teach-ers throughout the United States, but teens held most of the leadership roles on the island and helped determine the direction of the project. Through Eye4YouAlliance, library staff held meetings, hosted virtual games and events, and streamed library-related media on a weekly basis for any interested patrons, teens or otherwise.

While the Eye4YouAlliance was initially popular—island traffic peaked at the annual college fair of 2007 with 10,988 visitors—we soon faced prob-lems with funding and technology requirements. High maintenance costs and a lack of branch computers capable of running Second Life took a toll on the project, and by the college fair of 2008, visitation numbers had dropped to 200. With a traffic vacuum compounding its other difficulties, Eye4YouAlliance was taken offline in 2009.

Eye4YouAlliance is just one example of a cutting-edge library service that, while valuable, proved to be unsupportable in the long term. As Frank Blair, director of research, innovation, and strategy, puts it, "Anything new is going to fail to work some of the time. If it is truly uncharted territory, then no one has mapped out all the ways it can fail. We are bound to find at least some of them" (Blair 2009). Therefore, in the face of difficulty or even failure, the Library has continued to endure and improve its methods.

Projects are constantly added, removed, and changed in the pursuit of the best forum to connect with teens. All of our work, effective or not, has led to the current social networking model, and all the success it enjoys.

THE FORUM: CURRENT CONNECTIONS AT CHARLOTTE MECKLENBURG LIBRARY

Currently, Charlotte Mecklenburg Library is embracing a variety of social networking technologies in an effort to stay connected with teens. The Library has nearly 5,000 friends (MySpace), fans (Facebook), and followers (Twitter) combined. We have encountered many challenges as we continue to experiment, but we have also experienced great successes along the way. What we know for sure is that there is always room for improvement.

Knowing that there is still much to be learned from MySpace and You-Tube, we are still deeply invested in these technologies. Meebo and Flickr also continue to provide us with positive outcomes for teens. We have also added Facebook and Twitter to our repertoire. While we see the potential in both Facebook and Twitter, we're still experimenting with them as we look for the most constructive and meaningful ways to reach and connect with teens using these social networking technologies.

While Meebo isn't being used heavily on a daily basis in all of our branches, the ongoing availability of IM chat reference through the Library's teen website, where virtual questions are fielded by Loft staff, continues to be a success. What makes Meebo especially successful is the ease with which it enables teens to have a positive interaction with the library. All Loft staffers recognize the user name of one teen in particular because she sends messages through Meebo so often:

> She sends us a message a few times a week to ask about good books to read, fun websites to check out, or fun things to do in Charlotte. It seems that she just likes that she can contact us and have a little conversation when she is bored. In this way, she is learning that libraries and library staff can provide useful and fun resources for her. (Wyckoff 2009)

It is not only important for the library to take steps to meet teens on their level but also crucial to make teens feel welcome visiting the library—whether in person or virtually. If teens feel too intimidated to walk into a library and approach a librarian at a reference desk with a question, we want them to know that they can use something like Meebo to contact us electronically.

MySpace Evolution

Even though MySpace was the first social networking tool embraced by the Library, we are still trying to make it relevant for our teens 3 years later. Of all of the MySpace pages created by the Library, The Loft's page is by far the most popular. However, MySpace has begun to lose value at many of the other library branches. Some branches never even created a page primarily because there was not enough time or resources or there was no real demand for one. Other branches created MySpace pages several years ago and eventually stopped updating them because their teens were simply not interested. Matt Roach, teen librarian, explains that "the lack of interest warrants no time spent to invest on updating the page. After working very hard on a MySpace page for years and [despite] having it nationally noticed, it never did any good. Very few teens ever visited it, and it was a lot of work to continually update it" (Roach 2009). A couple of branches give their teen volunteers the task of updating their MySpace pages because teens are familiar with the site, have the needed skills, and are interested in participating in this way.

For the most part, however, it appears that MySpace has not had much staying power for our neighborhood and regional branches. This is likely due to the fluctuating nature of social networking sites themselves. The Library's MySpace pages are on the decline, at least in part, because Facebook has overtaken MySpace as the world's largest online social network (DiSalvo 2010; Roa 2009). Offering more advanced and accessible digital spaces, sites such as Facebook and Twitter have captured a sizable amount of current social networking traffic, a consequence that Ervin believes is due to MySpace's inability to keep up with evolving trends: "When you compare MySpace to the other options as far as setting up a digital place, the customization is there, but [MySpace] lacks intuitive and easy setup features" (Ervin 2009).

Capitalizing on the Popularity of Facebook

Since Facebook has gained popularity, libraries are trying to capitalize on this trend—our library included. Eleven of our branches have Facebook pages, including The Loft and the Library's main page. We know we can attract more teens to our Facebook pages and keep their interest by offering them something relevant to their needs and interests. As Catherine Haydon, teen specialist at The Loft, recommends: "Even something as simple as having a Shelfari or Goodreads application on a library's

Facebook is another way of providing reader's advisory services to connect with teens" (Haydon 2009).

Another way to offer teens something useful is to invite them to events using Facebook. This is better than an outdated e-mail reminder, but it is not a guaranteed form of communication. Karyn Jester, library services specialist, uses Facebook to connect with the Teen Advisory Council at her branch: "All of our communications with our teen advisory committee start with Facebook" (Jester 2009).

The biggest obstacle we face is motivating teens to "friend" or "fan" us. As Wyckoff points out: "We have tried to advertise our profile pages, but teens don't seem to want to friend the library. Teens may be checking out our profile, but not too many of them are actually adding us as friends. Many of our friends are other librarians and library professionals" (Wyckoff 2009).

We're currently working on new ways to add value to our Facebook presence so that we might better interest and engage teens. As Seth Ervin, teen specialist at The Loft, said:

> We have got to push our social networking capabilities to somehow render a tangible value to young adults. They won't participate in something just for the sake of doing it, but they will participate in something that is intrinsically worthwhile for them. (Ervin 2009)

Devising new and innovative ways of encouraging teens to add us on these social networking sites is one of our continued goals. For now, we are spreading the word by talking to teens who attend our library programs. If they friend us, their friends are more likely to do so as well. Wyckoff projects:

> We are hoping to have a revamped teen services website this year, which we hope to be able to showcase a link to our Facebook and MySpace pages. We think more teens will be visiting the new site and therefore also our social networking pages. (Wyckoff 2010)

Looking at Twitter

Twitter is another trend that holds promise for our library. Currently, only a quarter of the Library's branches are using this technology to try to connect with patrons, and most tweets are not aimed directly at teens but at library patrons in general. This is a reflection of the fact that teens are not using it to the same extent as they do other social networking sites.

The handful of branches that are using Twitter are taking advantage of applications that enable the administrator to update multiple profiles simultaneously, resulting in a more streamlined online presence. Right now, Wyckoff observes little teen use of Twitter and touches on the importance of knowing the teens you serve:

> It is important that the staff member who maintains the page has a good relationship with the teens in the community so that he or she can determine what type of content interests those specific teens. In addition, that staff member will be able to determine which sites teens are using. For example, we now have a Twitter page but do not see teens using Twitter at The Loft. For this reason, we are still focusing on encouraging teens to friend us on MySpace and Facebook. (Wyckoff 2009)

Until we see more teens on Twitter, we'll continue using it to reach parents, educators, and other adults.

On the other hand, Flickr continues to be a useful tool, not only for promotion and teen involvement but also as a source of dynamic content for the Library's various social networking profiles. Flickr photo streams frequently appear on library blogs, and photos from the Flickr account will be a part of the upcoming website redesign process. We continue to find new functions for YouTube as well, for entertainment and educational purposes. Russ Reed, technology specialist at ImaginOn, explains how powerful this technology is: "YouTube is not just a video hosting service. It's a forum where each video can be commented on by anybody who watches it, and viewers can even make 'video responses' to the video they just watched" (Reed 2009). YouTube remains valuable because it exercises critical thinking skills and promotes interaction rather than consumption. The Library is also experimenting with other visual social media, such as Scratch, which allows users to create and share simple games and animations.

The Continuing Success of Blogs

Blogs may seem outdated compared to the other social networking technologies that are popular right now, but we have found that they are still helping us reach teens at a few of our branches. For the most part, these blogs contain information about the library and the programming that is offered at each branch. One blog uses the Shelfari widget to display books that the teen librarian has recently read. Similarly, other branches use Goodreads for this purpose as well as encouraging teen patrons to create their own accounts. Some examples of blogs with teen-focused content include the Teen Writers Blog at the Morrison Regional Branch, the Teen Corner at the University City Regional Branch, and the Freedom Teens Blog at the Freedom Regional Branch.

Certainly, we do not claim to have it all figured out just yet. However, we do remain deliberate in our experimentation with the goal of creating sites and tools that offer our teens something substantial and worthwhile. Ervin makes a valid point: "I feel at its current state it is still in an experimental stage of seeing how to craft these media to serve our patrons. Over the years I believe that the Library will be able to become very efficient as we use these tools through experimenting with them so early" (Ervin 2009).

NETWORK MIGRATION: WHAT'S NEXT FOR SOCIAL NETWORKING AT CHARLOTTE MECKLENBURG LIBRARY

Taking its place as a forerunner of innovative programs and services for teens, Charlotte Mecklenburg Library continues to push forward in connecting with teens through technology. The challenge that we face when it comes to teens and social networking is to take the foundation of what has been done and continue to build upon it for the future:

> In the future I think our social media presence must be both embedded and distributed throughout our customers' own social media experience. The social networking tools that our customers use in their everyday life will not, in many cases, be those owned or operated by the library, but presences owned or operated by the customer or a third party. We must find ways to distribute our presence, rather than spin our wheels trying to drive everything to a library owned and operated website or blog. (Blair 2009)

Technology is always changing. To keep up with it we must be prepared to seek out new trends constantly while evaluating the true impact of measures already in place.

One way in which we're trying to maximize the use of our distributed online presence is by redesigning the Library's teen website. The current site is outdated and offers minimal capabilities. With our new website, we hope to have more control over the content and to integrate the various social networking technologies that we're already using. Ideas for the new website include adding Facebook Connect, pulling photos from our Flickr account, and offering more dynamic and location-specific content.

Beck Buck, a teen specialist who has been instrumental in the website redesign, explains the process:

> We take advantage of Word Press and shared content plug-ins to build a modular website that we, as librarians, have more control over. The website can be a place that draws all of our separate Web presences together under one virtual roof. Rather than just linking to different accounts, we try to embed dynamic pieces of those accounts wherever possible—for example, displaying a branch's current Facebook status and a rotation of its most recent pictures on Flickr. (Buck 2009)

The continued popularity of MySpace, Facebook, and Twitter certainly provides encouragement for the Library to continue using these media to help draw teens into branches. As long as teens use these sites to keep in touch with each other, they will continue to be places where libraries can put information with the hope that teens will see it. We also hope to get more teen involvement in blogging and podcasting to give an authentic teen voice to the Library's offerings in these venues. This could be a great opportunity not only to engage teens in helping promote the library but also to educate them on the technical aspects of creating and maintaining a successful blog or podcast channel.

In addition, cell phones are an increasingly important tool for teens and communication. Keeping this in mind, the Library's teen-serving staff members are beginning to develop new ideas for using Short Message Service (SMS) technology to begin offering program announcements and notices about available or overdue books via text messages sent through teens' phones. The new teen website will also offer the opportunity to sign up for an RSS feed that will give teens automatic updates on new information posted to the website.

The Library has also begun experimenting with Wiki and IdeaTorrent formats for internal staff use to share ideas and knowledge across the system. The results have been promising so far. Some of the best suggestions for cost savings during an extremely challenging budget planning process came from IdeaTorrent. The success of this project indicates likely future success in using these media for the systemwide sharing of ideas and experiences relating to teen services. Additionally, since patron input is a key part of planning and implementing successful library services, opening up idea-sharing tools such as these to patrons, including teens, would create a new method in which patrons could offer input on what they would like to see at their library.

The future will also mean looking past what the Library can create on its own to ways in which we can encourage and foster library participation in community-established networks. While there will always be a place for websites owned and operated by the library, participation on nonlibrary platforms is key to the distribution of our social media presence. This could take the form of partnerships with prominent community-run technologies such as school websites, Nings, and smaller, localized social networks.

Even with as much as we have going on now, we still see more on the horizon for the Library, and we will make every effort to be ready for new tools and trends as they become available. Whatever social networks teens use next, we will work to incorporate them at the Library as part of our ongoing work to connect with teens. In support of our library's mission, vision, and goals, we strive not only to keep up with emerging trends but also to lead the way. We hope that what we share with you will help you get your library successfully connected with teens.

SAVE AS: SUGGESTIONS FOR BEST PRACTICES FROM AN AWARD-WINNING LIBRARY

There are no hard and fast rules that will make implementing social networking technologies at your library a quick and simple process, but we have compiled a list of best practices that we hope will make it a little easier for you. No matter what the differences or similarities might be between Charlotte Mecklenburg Library and your library, these suggestions can be used as a springboard for implementing social networking with teens in a way that will suit your library's needs.

Listen to Teens

Getting teens actively involved in the planning, implementation, and evaluation process is always a key part of teen services, and it's especially crucial when applied to the ever-changing trends of social networking. Reed points out that while adults like to make careful plans, when it comes to what teens want to hear and know, trying to plan too much can be counterproductive: "We can't afford to stop listening to, and watching, our teens. They're the ones who'll tell us what's best suited. If they're not interested in it, it's a waste of time and effort" (Reed 2009). Look at what social networks teens are using in your library, and offer programs that will enhance their experience—page layout workshops, digital photography sessions, etc. Pay special attention to the teen response—or lack of teen response—to your social networking efforts, and adjust your approach as needed.

Other practical ways to get teen input about social networking include creating a short survey to find out what social media they're using or employing a teen volunteer to maintain the library's social networking presence. As Wyckoff reminds us,

> Word-of-mouth is the best way to market the library social networking profiles, so if a teen volunteer or regular at the library finds the profile interesting or useful, he or she might encourage his or her friends to check out the library's profiles also. (Wyckoff 2009)

Listen to Colleagues

As with any other aspect of library services, it's important to share experiences and findings with colleagues. Social networking tools can be just as useful for teen-serving staff as they are for teens. While they can be used for one person to share information with many, these tools are also ideal for eliciting responses and conversations about that shared information. This conversation based on the exchange of information through blogs, photos, video uploads, and other sources will not only keep staff informed but also encourage participation, and added voices will enhance the product being delivered to teens. Finally, collaboration can free up staff time, prevent burnout, and help with project continuity in the event of staff changes.

Lobby for Social Networking Technologies at Your Library

Administrative support has been tremendously helpful to the Library's continuing social networking efforts. If your library system does not support its staff in implementing social networking technologies, you have additional hurdles to overcome. In fact, some libraries block social networking sites altogether from their computer terminals. If this happens to be the case at your library, it might be up to you to advocate for social networking with teens. Take some time to do your research and build a strong case. You'll find allies among librarians who have been in similar situations and librarians who have had success with social networking. First, you will want to identify the resources you'll need to engage in social networking so that the staff impact will be clear. Also, you must present research showing how social networking can contribute positively to adolescent development and how libraries are using these sites to connect with teens. In this way, patron outcomes will be evident to decision makers. And remember,

> Just because the library blocks the sites within its walls doesn't mean joining these sites—as your library, as a librarian, or as yourself—won't have an impact on your community. Being available to those using the services may still have the effect you're looking for. (Vieau 2009)

Keep Teens Aware of Safety Risks while Still Encouraging Creativity

While encouraging teens to engage in social networking and to express themselves by creating content using social media, be sure to make safety a priority. The Library strongly encourages youth to think carefully about what kind of information they make public, what they say to others online, and especially what they say in audio and video content that they upload to the Internet. Reed asserts that awareness of online safety risks is already common sense for a growing number of teens:

> Tools like YouTube aren't a new thing to teens as much as they are to adults. They're just another part of their world, like refrigerators and homework....But sometimes [teens] just don't understand how risky it can really be, and it is everybody's responsibility, from the library to the living room, to promote and explain Internet safety in a way that the kids will understand. (Reed 2009)

Many social networking tools already have an age requirement. For instance, a person is supposed to be 13 years old to register with YouTube, MySpace, or Facebook. Of course rules don't always prevent younger teens from using social networks, so be sure to mention any safety concerns that arise when using social media with teens of any age, and stay up to date with the rules and privacy policies of the various types of social networks. This will also enable you to address parental concerns.

Additionally, you might create standards for social networking at your library. The Library created MySpace standards to help with uniformity and to help staff create developmentally appropriate pages for teens. These standards also included accepting only friend requests from teens, other libraries or librarians, local youth-serving organizations, and YA authors.

Fear Not!

Above all, don't be afraid to try new things! Much of the Library's success with social networking can be attributed to our willingness to take risks.

> Developing and implementing cutting-edge library services such as social networking requires staff and administration to take risks, try new things, occasionally fail spectacularly, evaluate, and learn from our mistakes in order to do it all over again, often more effectively the second, third, and fourth times. (Gorman 2009)

If your first efforts at social networking with teens at the library aren't successful, reevaluate your goals and your assumptions about your audience, listen to what teens are (or in some cases, aren't) saying, and try it from another angle.

Engaging in social networking with teens also means embracing change. While sustainability is a good long-term goal, sometimes just being timely is enough. For instance, by the time this book is published, many of the social networks that are popular among teens now may be forgotten for newer types of social media. Sometimes it can be difficult to let go of a comfortable and familiar tool. But social media is teaching us that even if it's uncomfortable at first, adaptation is important because communication is expanding exponentially. "In the end, we're all just standing in a big room with zillions of other people, trying to be heard, and it's very, very exciting" (Reed 2009). Social networking provides an opportunity not just for librarians to try new things and to meet teens where they are but also an opportunity for teens to communicate in a new way, to get them out of their shells, and to let them see what the whole world thinks about what they have to say.

CONCLUSION

According to David Singleton, Charlotte Mecklenburg Library's director of library experiences:

> Social media space allows for two-way conversation in a world in which personal connections are becoming less frequent and more cherished. In our organization, staff are encouraged to think creatively about how we can best serve users, and [staff] are empowered to implement innovative programs and services that align with our strategic goals. Because our staff are encouraged to be in social

media spaces, where the users are, we have an opportunity to connect personally in ways that might be challenging in the traditional library environment. (Singleton 2009)

At Charlotte Mecklenburg Library, we're proud of the social networking connections we've made with teens, and we hope that sharing our experience—the successes and the failures—will benefit all libraries seeking to connect with teens.

REFERENCES

Blair, Frank. (December 18, 2009). E-mail message to authors.

Buck, Beck. (December 18, 2009). E-mail message to authors.

DiSalvo, David. "Are Social Networks Messing with Your Head?" *Scientific American Mind* (January 2010): 48–55.

Ervin, Seth. (December 18, 2009). E-mail message to authors. (January 13, 2010). Federal Trade Commission. "Social Networking Sites: Safety Tips for Tweens and Teens." 2006, http://www.ftc.gov/bcp/edu/pubs/consumer/tech/tec14.shtm/ (accessed March 27, 2010).

Gorman, Michele. (December 18, 2009). E-mail message to authors.

Haydon, Catherine. (December 18, 2009). E-mail message to authors.

Jester, Karyn. (December 18, 2009). E-mail message to authors.

Reed, Russ. (December 18, 2009). E-mail message to authors.

Roa, Leena. "The Gap Grows Wider: MySpace Eats Facebook's Dust in the U.S." *Techcrunch,*July 13, 2009, http://www.techcrunch.com/2009/07/13/the-gap-grows-wider-myspace-eats-facebooks-dust-in-the-us/ (accessed March 27, 2010). Roach, Matt. (December 18, 2009). E-mail message to authors.

Singleton, David. (December 18, 2009). E-mail message to authors.

Vieau, Jesse. (December 18, 2009). E-mail message to authors. (January 25, 2010). Wyckoff, Amy. (December 18, 2009). Email message to authors. (January 17, 2010).

WEBSITES

Charlotte Mecklenburg Library main page, http://www.facebook.com/cmlibrary/

Charlotte Mecklenburg Library's teen website, http://www.libraryloft.org/

Flickr stream, http://www.flickr.com/photos/libraryloft/

Freedom Regional Branch, http://freedomteens.blogspot.com/

Library Loft, www.libraryloft.org/

Loft at ImaginOn's MySpace page, http://www.myspace.com/libraryloft/

Morrison Regional Branch, http://gamwich.blogspot.com/

University City Regional Branch, http://ucrlibrary.wordpress.com/teen-corner/

12

◇ ◇ ◇

BRINGING IT ALL TOGETHER: WHAT DOES IT MEAN FOR LIBRARIANS WHO SERVE TEENS?

June Abbas and Denise E. Agosto

WHAT DOES IT ALL MEAN FOR LIBRARIES?

Teens + Social Networks + Libraries = ? A win–win situation? An opportunity for adapting our thinking about what constitutes a library and library services to teens? Or do libraries choose not to engage with teens in social networks because of concerns about legal and ethical ramifications or privacy and safety issues, or because it is simply too time-consuming and requires that we learn new technical skills? These issues and potential barriers are important for certain, but what about the benefits to teens and to libraries? These important considerations were explored in depth throughout this book.

We also presented many creative, innovative, and useful ideas for engaging teens and providing library services using different social networking technologies. Through practice and research-based discussions we learned more about the types of social networks being used by teens and why, and the advantages (social, developmental, educational, and technical) as well as the disadvantages of each. We have also outlined some of the most recent research on teens and social networks and how libraries are using them to provide services to teens, tempering these experiences with cautionary tales, best practices, and general advice for how to start using social networking with teens in your library. We hope that you found each chapter inspiring and found many ideas that you cannot wait to try in your own library.

As noted in the Introduction, we found in our research that public libraries can benefit from the use of social networking technologies with teens in a three major ways: (1) by broadening the reach of the library's young adult (YA) programs and services; (2) by enabling the library to better support teens' healthy social development; and (3) by facilitating opportunities for public librarians to teach teens how to engage in safer online interactions (Agosto and Abbas 2009). This book has explained each of these three categories of benefits in more detail and has described specific ways that public librarians can obtain these benefits for their libraries, as well as addressing potential drawbacks. So many wonderful ideas, best practices, and tips for use were provided by the authors of the book that it is difficult to list them all here. What we provide instead is first an overall profile of how, and more importantly why, teens use social networking technologies and the social, developmental, educational, and technical benefits they derive from their use. Second, we present best practice ideas for library services that we have gleaned from reviewing the chapters related to (1) the design of social networking tools for libraries, (2) services to teens, and (3) advocacy.

A PROFILE OF TEENS' USE OF SOCIAL NETWORKING TECHNOLOGIES

- In thinking about technology, teens don't separate social networking technologies from other technologies like cell phones and texting—it's all about communication! Also, social networking sites no longer support just using one mode of communication. Sites like Facebook and MySpace include widgets for blogs, RSS feeds, picture and video uploading, surveys and quizzes, reviews, tags, and more.

- Teens choose their communication media based on a number of contextual factors (the relationship with the intended message recipients and with the number of intended recipients) as well as based on simplicity of use, speed of communication, the ability to maintain constant contact, and multitasking capabilities.

- Most teens read constantly—text messages, e-mail, MySpace and Facebook, magazines, instant messages, and websites—as well as required school reading and books.

- Teens like to multitask and use multiple different social networks and Web 2.0 applications, sometimes concurrently and for different reasons, such as to relieve boredom.

- Teens need things that make them feel successful socially. They need to feel that they have friends and are liked, and social networking sites can fulfill this need.

- Teens use social networks to find out who they are and to become more comfortable with themselves. Social networking technologies allow them to experiment or "try on" different identities.

- Social networks provide safe spaces for teens to ask questions and facilitate problem solving, thereby exploring topics of interest that they may not feel comfortable talking about face to face.

- What teens need to develop successfully is a combination of social and emotional developmental support as well as an array of technological skills. Social networking sites aid teens in becoming fluent in the use of technology in a way that is natural and integrated into their lives. Teens develop the technological fluency they will need to survive in the 21st century workplace and society when they learn to use the multiple social networking applications, create content, and participate in social networks.

- Teens are no longer just knowledge consumers but now also knowledge producers (demonstrating expertise through weblogs, fan sites, and videos). Social networking websites have, in fact, helped to create an online culture where the teens create and share content and all members participate in content creation and distribution.

BEST PRACTICE IDEAS FOR LIBRARY SERVICES
The Design of Social Networking Tools for Libraries

Get Teens Involved

The importance of involving teens in the development of the library's social networking tools cannot be overstated. The real experts of teens' thoughts and behaviors are teens themselves, and the best way to keep library services relevant to teens' evolving interests and behaviors is to create formal and informal avenues for the ongoing collection of teen input, such as teen advisory boards, teen idea and design teams, periodic surveys, informal focus groups, volunteering and internship opportunities, and other informal conversations with teens.

Keep It Simple but Visible

Simplicity, visibility, and speed of access are key for engaging teens' interest and participation. Librarians should make sure that their online services are easy for teens to use, contact information is easy to find, there are links to and between different sites, and that their social networking pages are not overly cluttered or overwhelming to navigate.

Use Multiple Technologies

Librarians should use multiple social networking tools to promote their services, trying out different social networking technologies to see what works best. Rather than using a social networking page to promote just one activity or information medium, librarians should provide teens with a variety of online activity choices, including activities that can be undertaken simultaneously.

Don't Abandon Tools That Work

Librarians should not abandon e-mail contact with teens in favor of social networks but rather use both contact methods. Give teens a choice for how they wish to communicate with their libraries and their librarians.

Keep Sites Up to Date and Fresh

The content provided via these tools must be kept up to date and visible. Library pages must be updated frequently and fresh content provided. Post announcements of programs and events, pictures of past programs, teen advisory boards, and so on. Give teens multiple opportunities to contribute, as through blogs, book and media reviews, collaborations with other teens and librarians, and so on. Keep the content current and engaging.

Be Proactive

Create official standards to use in creating library social networking tools, including guidelines such as consistent tagging, updated schedules, who is allowed to post and update content, and restrictions to friend requests. In this way you have to review what you are doing and what is working or not working, but you also will keep up to date on legal considerations and the expectations of your staff, administration, and community.

Change When Needed

The use of these multiple technologies to reach teens can remain effective only if librarians are willing to be flexible and to change as teens' uses and preferences change. Be prepared to move to new social networking technologies as new social networks and even new technologies emerge and as teens adopt them.

Services to Teens

Be Visible

Meet teens where they are—whether it is on a blog, a website, an online book group, YouTube, Facebook, or Twitter. Find out the technologies your teens use most frequently and use these as a guide to where and how you decide to promote library services. Teens still need to feel a personal connection with the library and librarian.

Take Your Library Services and Programs to Teens

Online library services to teens should complement but not replace face-to-face services, and librarians should consider how instruction and services can be offered as hybrids, to teens via cell phones, or via other mobile devices.

Promote Your Services

Many teens are more willing to join library pages on Facebook and other social networks than they are willing to friend their librarians. This makes organizational social networking pages ideal tools for providing teens with information about library services, the library's teen website, upcoming program announcements, blurbs promoting new book and media acquisitions, contact points for homework assistance, and more. Also, promote your social networking tools on your library and teen web pages, in library newsletters, and on posters in the library and places where teens hang out, such as coffee shops. Don't forget traditional methods of promotion.

Innovate Traditional Practices

One of the roles of the YA librarian has always been to find ways of connecting teens with YA literature. Libraries can use social networks to meet this challenge in a number of ways: social networking sites such as Facebook and MySpace; blogs; bulletins; library web pages; video book reviews or book trailers; online book clubs or literature circles; Second Life and other 3D social worlds; book sharing sites such as Shelfari, Goodreads or LibraryThing; RSS feeds; and Twitter. Keep in mind other traditional practices that you can bring alive by using social networks and other new and emerging technologies.

Create a Culture of Social Learning

Rather than creating a culture of fear by focusing on the negative aspects of social networks and the law, design educational programs that stress the rights and responsibilities of Internet use. Teens must learn how to make good choices in social networking situations, and librarians can teach teens about their rights regarding copyright, privacy, reporting cyberbullying and/or stalking, and making good choices online.

Be a Role Model of Good Digital Citizenship

It's essential that today's librarians promote and model legal and ethical technology practices. Educating young people about their rights and responsibilities as digital citizens is also a role that librarians can play.

Keep Your Technology Skills and Knowledge Current

The best way to do this is simply to use these tools. Try new applications and see what works. Read the literature and research about teens and social networking. Attend professional development workshops or develop them for your community.

Share Your Success—and Failure—Stories with Colleagues

Write about them, blog about them, talk about them. Get the word out about how you use social networking with teens or why you *don't* do so.

Advocacy

Be an Advocate for Teens

It is still difficult for some parents and educators to recognize that social networks are more than just "social." Besides enabling teens to work on their reading and writing skills, social networking sites also provide teens with opportunities to create, collaborate, grow socially and emotionally, and develop technological fluency. Librarians can serve as advocates for teens by providing more information to teens' communities (parents, teachers, and other key players in teens' everyday life experiences) about the social, developmental, and educational benefits of social networking.

Help Lift Access Barriers

Libraries and librarians can help to balance teens' rights to access information and use social networking sites with the wishes of parents and teachers to protect their children from harm. Librarians can help to lift access barriers by developing programs for parents and forming collaborations with teachers and administrators and other library professionals with the goal of educating each other about the benefits of providing access to social networking technologies.

Provide Access to the Technology

Provide access to computers and social networking sites in your library. Teens may not have access to computers at home, so that libraries and schools may be their main sources of access.

Keep Your Library's Acceptable Use Policy (AUP) Up to Date and Make Sure That It Complies with Local, State, and Federal Regulations

Updating the AUP provides librarians with a great learning opportunity to keep current on new legislation as well as to consider the role of new technologies in library services. Design a policy focusing on positive statements that stress intellectual freedom, safe behavior, education, and social responsibility.

CONCLUSION

Nearly all of these suggestions for best practices are contingent on talking with teens to learn about their evolving ideas and behaviors. As is the case with more traditional library services for teens, we must makes teens' voices central to the design and delivery of library services via social networks and other social media by talking with them on an ongoing basis. Most of all, don't be afraid to try new things. If something doesn't work, finding out that it failed is one way to learn what not to do next time. It is also an opportunity to learn more about how your library can effectively use social networking technologies with teens.

REFERENCE

Agosto, Denise E., and June Abbas. "Teens and Social Networking: How Public Libraries Are Responding to the Latest Online Trend." *Public Libraries* 48 (2009): 32–37.

INDEX

ABOUT THE EDITORS AND CONTRIBUTORS

JUNE ABBAS, Ph.D., is an associate professor in the School of Library and Information Studies, College of Arts and Sciences, at the University of Oklahoma. Her research interests include the use of technologies by children and youth, their information use behaviors, and the design of age-appropriate systems for youth. Dr. Abbas has presented and published widely on children and technology, user-centered design for youth and teens, and the societal impacts of children and youth's Internet use in public libraries.

DENISE E. AGOSTO, Ph.D., is an associate professor at the College of Information Science and Technology at Drexel University. Her research interests include public libraries, diversity issues in youth library services, youth information behaviors, and gender and information behavior. Dr. Agosto has published many articles and book chapters in these areas and has received multiple awards for her research and teaching. Most recently she coauthored, with Sandra Hughes-Hassell, Ph.D., *Urban Teens in the Library: Research and Practice* (American Library Association, 2010).

ELIZABETH BURNS is the youth services consultant for the New Jersey State Library Talking Book and Braille Center. She coauthored, with Sophie Brookover, *Pop Goes the Library: Using Pop Culture to Connect with*

Your Whole Community (Information Today, 2008). Ms. Burns writes and presents about pop culture and fan fiction. She can be found online writing about books, movies, and pop culture at her website, *A Chair, A Fireplace & A Tea Cozy* (yzocaet.blogspot.com).

BELINHA S. DE ABREU, Ph.D., is an assistant teaching professor in the College of Information Science and Technology at Drexel University. Her research interests include media literacy education, new media, information literacy, critical thinking, young adults, and teacher training. Dr. De Abreu's focus is on the impact and learning as a result of media watched and used by K–12 students. Most recently, she published "Middle Schoolers, Media Literacy, & Methodology: The Three M's," in *Issues in Information and Media Literacy: Education, Practice and Pedagogy*, 2009.

CHRISTEN HIGGINS is a library service specialist I with the Charlotte Mecklenburg Library. Her love of literature and technology is rivaled only by her love of sharing it with anyone who will listen, especially children and teens.

JANET HILBUN, Ph.D., is an assistant professor at the University of North Texas in Denton, Texas, where she teaches children's and young adult literature courses. She has an MLS from Texas Woman's University and a Ph.D. in library and information science from Rutgers. In her "former lives," she taught high school and middle school English and reading and was a middle school librarian. She is the coauthor, with Jane Claes, of *Coast to Coast: Exploring State Book Awards* (Libraries Unlimited, 2010).

ANNETTE LAMB, Ph.D., is an online professor at the School of Library and Information Science at Indiana University at Indianapolis. Her research interests include educational technology, school librarianship, graphic inquiry, and issues related to social technology and youth. Dr. Lamb's numerous articles and over a dozen books focus on realistic approaches to technology integration and information inquiry for youth. Most recently, she coauthored, with Daniel Callison, *Graphic Inquiry* (Libraries Unlimited, 2010).

ERIC M. MEYERS is an instructor at the School of Library, Archival, and Information Studies at the University of British Columbia. He is completing his doctorate in information science at the University of Washington. He holds master's degrees in information science and education from the University of Michigan and Stanford University, respectively. Eric's research interests lie at the intersection of information science, the learning sciences, and new media studies. His work examines the information practices of young people in academic and everyday contexts.

REBECCA PIERSON is a librarian with Teen Services at Charlotte Mecklenburg Library. A graduate of the University of North Carolina School of Information and Library Science, she's thrilled any time she can connect teens with the library, whether it's through reading, programming, or social networking.

SEAN RAPACKI received his bachelor's degree from the University of Chicago, where he studied literature and psychology. He received his master's degree from the Kent State University School of Library and Information Science. His life has led him to gigs as a carnie, a professional musician, a freelance journalist, and a salesman of mortuary refrigerators, but he is currently the teen librarian at Wadsworth Public Library. He resides in Ohio with his wife, stepchildren, and dog.

STEPHANIE D. REYNOLDS, Ph.D. is an assistant professor at School of Library and Information Science, University of Kentucky, where she teaches courses in children's literature, young adult literature, and youth services. Dr. Reynolds has a master's of science degree in library science, specializing in youth librarianship, and a Ph.D. in interdisciplinary information science, both from the University of North Texas. Her primary research areas are the bibliocognitive and bibliotherapeutic aspects of young adult literature and the response to literature in social networks.

HOLLY SUMMERS is a teen services librarian with Charlotte Mecklenburg Library. She received her MLS from the State University of New York at Buffalo, and she is interested in finding new and exciting ways to connect with teens through innovative programming and services.

JOYCE KASMAN VALENZA, Ph.D., is the teacher librarian at Springfield Township High School in Erdenheim, PA. For ten years, she was the techlife@school columnist for the *Philadelphia Inquirer*. Joyce is the author of *Power Tools, Power Research Tools*, and *Power Tools Recharged* for ALA Editions. She currently blogs for *School Library Journal* and writes for a variety of other edtech journals. Joyce speaks nationally about issues relating to libraries and the thoughtful use of educational technology.

RALPH WOODRING is a library service associate at Charlotte Mecklenburg Library. After graduating from the University of North Carolina at Charlotte, his passion for literature set him on the path to helping others at the library. When he is not helping teens find that perfect new story, he may be seen scribbling into one of many notebooks, trying to clear a path for the next generation of readers.